A Relationship Guide:

Love, Sex & Everything In Between

Greg Dudzinski, MS, LPC

A Relationship Guide:

Love, Sex & Everything In Between

Please note: the author is a licensed professional counselor in the State of Michigan. This book is not a replacement for marriage, couples, or individual counseling. It is intended for self-help purposes and is forewarned that any actions taken by the reader is the sole responsibility of said reader. The author or any associated party cannot be held liable.

ISBN 13: 978-0-578-82700-1

Published by: The Art of Relationships, PLLC,

Detroit, MI

Dedication

I continue to be forever grateful in providing updated materials and new insights in book edition. There literally is not a day that passes, where I am amazed at the many couples and individuals in the world striving with all of their hearts and souls to have that fantastic, loving and deep relationship of a lifetime! Please continue your pursuits and remain proud! The love of a lifetime will come your way!

Love, Sex & Everything In Between continues to be dedicated to all the couples who have invited me into their private, emotional and personal lives over the years.

I am forever humbled that you chose me to help you move beyond your heartaches. Thank you! If it wasn't for you, I would not be able to reinforce and add additional helping principles. My passion continues in helping and learning from the many couples and individuals craving a terrific relationship! Thank you and much love!

I want to thank the relationship and marriage counseling pioneers and new pioneers that push the boundaries and challenge traditional methodologies and allow people to step outside the old school, biased and judgmental boxes. No individual or professional has endorsed this book. I will never mislead.

My passion is trying to help others reduce their own fears, insecurities and judgments placed upon them from a white, patriarchal, conservative and religious persecutory stance. Let's band together to stop racism and slanderous shaming of others!

Acknowledgments

I want to thank the countless couples and individuals that allowed me to enter their extremely private lives. I so wish you could all know how honored I am for that! You will never be taken for granted, Thank you!

A very special thank you to my forever love and daughter Shaylin, and to my unselfish parents, Jerry and Maryann.

Content

Part 4: Achieving Soulfulness

Introduction

Love, Sex & Everything In Between prides itself at helping you achieve the "Total Connection" in your love life. This is where the mind, body, heart and soul are intertwined into the relationship you've always desired!

I am flattered to be recognized as Detroit's Love Guru, and have written this book as a follow up or "improvement" to my first two books. Since I'm all about constant growth and improvement, I wanted to give readers more tools and thought-provoking insights to help improve their love lives. This book is dedicated to all of those who crave having a terrific, loving and passionate relationship! It's for the married, cohabiting, or those in a new relationship. PLUS, this is for the single people with hopes in finding and maintaining a fantastic and sexually fulfilling relationship!

I reiterate from my prior works: I do not use perfect English or grammar! And yes, I do swear on occasion. 😉 I get this will offend some, though I've learned a long time ago, I cannot please everyone. My style is prided on being real, genuine, compassionate, yet at the same time, a smart-ass and blunt at times. I tried writing this book, as I would be speaking to you in person. It's important for me to be genuine and not be fake, and will never present as an overly "professional" elitist. I will be interchanging *His* or *Her,* to reference gender aspects. No, I do not buy into all of one member of a given gender, being identical to another. Not all women are the same, and not all men are the same.

My goal is to bring insights and tools in helping you have a fantastic relationship. Clients, and some other professionals seeking my assistance, roll their eyes when I tell them: *"I'd love to help you feel more in love, more confident, plus deeper emotionally and physically than you have ever felt before! My desire is to help you be more connected than when you first started dating; even when you first got married!"* As you can see, (as many of you are as well) why so many couples roll their eyes after I make this statement! ;) Go ahead, be skeptical! I'm definitely okay with that! I've grown quite use to it over the years. Couples have even commented: "Greg, that's fucking impossible!" I just grin and simply ask: "Is it?" 😉

After reading this book, I firmly believe you will have a deeper, more passionate relationship than ever imagined! Though, let me be honest: if you don't implement the tools provided, nothing will improve….At the same time, I am hoping you will be more emotionally and sexually confident as an individual. I do wish I could guarantee this, though cannot. If you put in the work, and are able to look deeply into yourself and your relationship, there will be life changing gains! You can have that awesome connection you've always desired!

I will say this: if you are not willing to look into that proverbial mirror and explore yourself; if you are unwilling to take responsibility for your own growth and evolution in achieving that terrific, passionate and amazing relationship, then I advise you to not waste your time; you shouldn't be reading this. I told you; I can be blunt! :)

Are you ready to explore, grow and laugh too? Great! Take my hand as I help you have the relationship you've always craved. Here is Love, Sex & Everything In Between: A Relationship Guide.

PART 1: REALITIES of LOVE

Chapter 1: Expectations

During the very first session with a new couple, I often have them reflect and think about what their "expectations" are for a healthy, happy and passionate relationship. Sadly, there's often a blank look across their faces. "You know Greg, we haven't thought about that."

Seriously, I think most of us have had high hopes and expectations of relationship bliss and happiness. Along with these hopes, we search for our perfect "soul mate." Are soul mates really found, or are they actually made? I'll talk about these questions towards the end of the book. Though, this search begins with our expectations of what our ideal lover will be like.

During one of my show episodes, I talked about expectations and how crucial it is to have clear ones. No one is to remain in the dark, or caught off guard. Having clear expectations is a huge first step in having a peaceful relationship. How disagreements are handled and when the shit hits the fan (and it will!) are crucial elements that need to be discussed! It needs to happen before marriage or living together! Don't go into it thinking: *"Oh no problem, we'll handle those; no big deal!"* I'm going to tell you; they will become big deals and raise their ugly heads! It's just a matter of when, but they will! They surface when you least expect and at the worst possible times.

After 20 years of helping couples, I still get bewildered in hearing: *"Greg, we've never really had expectations."* This is the point where I begin teaching couples about true love, or perhaps the essence of love and relationships. It's not how I depict love or relationships; that'd be totally biased. It's about helping you build and meet your own relationship expectations.

How do you know if your partner, or potential partner will be right for you? I get it, the feelings of being in love, emotional highs and terrific sex surmount the thoughts of forever happiness! It engulfs your every breath. Though, not having any expectations is the start of the end for most relationships. This simply is being naïve or perhaps ignorant. Hey, I've been there myself! We think everything will be great forever and ever! Then, without warning, we start getting resentful when things don't work out as we expected. Here's the irony: because we had no idea what we expected in the first place. Or perhaps, more accurate is that we never shared our expectations with our loved one.

Our loved one's expectations start to creep out and often collide with our own. How our life expectations differ become contention points and tension builders. How these differences are handled are crucial, of course. Though, the major differences may never be able to be worked out.

Before you enter into a relationship, there exists YOU; just you! Your own thoughts, beliefs, values, likes, dislikes, you name it. Then all of a sudden you meet the love of your dreams and there's a tendency to forget all about YOU. What makes you happy, your personal dreams, hopes, and your life dreams drift to the background. I bet your loved one does the same thing. This is the infatuation part of love. These are the very things that will come back and bite you in the ass later.

Ultimately, these could shake your relationship to the core. I'm not talking about being selfish; not at all! It's about helping one another obtain their dreams and goals, plus feeling loved and appreciated as well. Of course, you should be receiving these very things from your lover in return!

You need an idea of what type of relationship you'd like, plus how you'd like it to be. Life does happen, and relationships are never perfect. Though, just blindly moving along will lead to huge disappointments for you both. Remember when everything was fantastic and "perfect?" What happened! ☺

It's still ironic how many people I talk to, either do not have any expectations for what a happy relationship resembles to them; or simply ignored them for the sake of their partner. As most are aware, this will lead to resentment and ultimately relationship demise. You need to discuss what it means to be happy in a relationship and within your selves! It's also wise to learn about one another and how they fit into your lifestyle, likes, dislikes, and ways of handling life. This is very hard to do when you are infatuated with one another and hold back your own wishes and dreams.

What are your expectations for happiness? This is a loaded question and very subjective. It could be one desires to travel the globe, while the other wants to sit home 80% of the time. One wants sex 5-7 days a week, and the other once a month. Have you even thought about the dynamics of parenting, sharing the bills, household duties, time with extended family, holiday traditions, and how you handle disagreements? I could go on and on… However, most people reading this book are already at the point where they are miserable and frustrated. This doesn't mean that expectations can't be renewed, expanded, or reinvented. They most certainly can! I have proof of these very things happening in my office daily. Expectations evolve!

A crucial note: some people, sadly, won't express their relationship desires or expectations for fear of rejection. Perhaps it's that their wishes will not be important to their partner. My question then becomes: why are you in that relationship?

It's also not fair that your lover isn't aware you become fearful or anxious when expressing yourself. They need to be made aware, plus given the opportunity to love you as you desire! Wouldn't you want your partner to express their ideas and what makes them happy? Without this knowledge, you have no concept how to meet their needs either. It's like traveling to a new destination without a map. You wouldn't even know which direction to start!

Please be open to expressing and learning what you both need to feel loved, desired, appreciated and respected. I listed a few areas above, that you can start talking about, plus identifying how you'd like to handle them. There's even a list sheet in the appendix at the back of this book. Please feel free to add to the list, in order to fit your own relationship needs!

Chapter 2: Relationship Myths

How many of you have fantasized about having the perfect relationship? Perhaps these are some of your expectations that weren't shared with your loved one. There'd be no yelling and screaming at one another; you'd be making passionate, toe-curling love every morning and night! You'd also be there for one another through chaos and setbacks! You would meet each other's needs and live forever happily into your graves......... Damn, was I just dreaming, or is this really possible? 😉

The great days are fantastic, though it's the shit days that will test your relationship and quickly challenge your so-called expectations. As your emotions flare, you may forget, or find that your original expectations are thrown out the window. However, keeping focused on your expectations will help you calm fired-up situations. By starting to learn your lover's true feelings, you will help center and reduce the anger while getting to the heart of the problem. More about this later.

I'm all about the concept that there is no perfect relationship. However, I also share a devotion in continuously chasing that perfection. Working together, and clearly expressing your expectations for a happy relationship is a paramount first step. Without talking about clear expectations and how you will deal with certain situations, you will be left grasping at thin air, trying to breathe to stay alive. Keeping expectations alive and in the forefront of your relationship takes discipline, as it does in many life goals. Remember, that as life grows, your expectations should evolve. Keep talking about them!

As soon as people (me included) hear the word DISCIPLINE we freak out, right? Like, oh shit, that's a bad, gut wrenching word! ☺ Perhaps it brings us back to our childhood in getting grounded, spanked, yelled at, or you name it. It takes discipline to keep learning about and striving towards healthy relationship expectations; both new and old alike. Plus, it takes discipline to have a terrific and loving relationship. I'm here to help ease the sting from the term: "*discipline*."

I'm going to flip that around. Can you use discipline as a good word, or perhaps a better phrase would be *self-driven*? Both terms represent the same meaning, though driven sounds like we are in control of our paths, versus others in control.

Many are driven in life areas such as careers and even parenting. I need to ask however: how many of you are driven to make your relationship great? It's both funny and sad at the same time; we are always waiting for our partners to "make us feel great." Though, I am prompting you *(okay, yelling at you LOL)* to become self-driven in making your lover feel loved, desired and cherished in forming a dynamic relationship! No more waiting for your lover to make the first move all the time! Be brave and take responsibility with your actions, while being driven towards your lover NOW! Start risking and finding out what your partner needs to feel loved, desired and cared for.

How can you expect your partner to meet your needs, if he doesn't feel your love in return? You may "expect" your partner needs X, Y and Z, while in fact he needs A, B and C. Your expectations of what your partner needs may be inaccurate. Start finding out the actual elements your Love truly needs and wants!

Are you self-driven to become the best lover you can be? Do you know what your lover really enjoys and makes her toes curl? Will you dare to be more sensual and sexual? Can you be more determined in becoming a better listener, more loving and understanding? Will you be more compassionate towards your lover? This doesn't mean your partner shouldn't return those favors. I highly encourage they do! Being self-driven promotes you taking control of yourself and what you want: this is a huge part in achieving happiness, plus acquiring the terrific relationship you desire. Don't just wait for it to happen, or you'll be waiting for unicorns to appear as well. 😊

The foundation is to start learning what your partner expects and desires in order to feel loved, desired, respected and important. These actions will also show that you actually care and give a shit! If your partner does not reciprocate in meeting your needs…well, I'll get into that later.

Being self-driven in the areas I presented above doesn't mean you are selling yourself out. I will never ever promote that! Fuck that! You deserve to be loved, craved, desired, respected, and to feel important in your relationship! What I am asking is that you be driven in becoming the best partner you can be, while at the same time, driven in your personal boundaries, goals and dreams and being the best YOU!

Chapter 3: The 3 Chemistries Explained

The total connection philosophy is based on these three "Chemistries. Simply, everyone has heard the term *Chemistry,* or "We just have so much Chemistry between us!" Okay, what the hell does this mean? LOL. Chemistry is also a form and interwoven aspect of expectations, plus compatibility. I'm going to do my best to break *Chemistry* down into three categories, or the 3 Chemistries.

First is the most obvious: *Physical Chemistry*. Most people want to find someone they are physically attracted to, plus have a partner who is also attracted to him/her. A simple no-brainer, right? Physical chemistry is subjective and as the age-old saying states: "Beauty is in the eye of the beholder." Physical attraction comes in all shapes and sizes, colors and creeds, as it should.

Some women like tall men, and some like short men. Some men like women with larger breasts, and some men could care less about breast size. The general attraction is what originally pulls us toward one another. This is true for most people, even for those who claim it doesn't matter. Forever, men have been referred to as shallow in the physical realms. I'm also here to inform you that women are pretty close as equally shallow. Even though physical chemistry is different for everyone; it seems to hold importance for most humans.

Another element that surrounds Physical Chemistry is the sexual realm. I'll cover this in more detail later on. A glimpse of *Sexual Chemistry* relies on physical pleasure and meeting one's sexual expectations. Being sexually desired and pleased is important for many people of any gender. On a deeper level, being sexually pleased and satisfied, is the essence of Physical Chemistry. Just because the physical attraction is there, doesn't dictate that the sexual chemistry will be. Do you disagree? This is where the other two Chemistries come into play.

Intellectual Chemistry also refers to the "Mind" aspect in my mind, body, heart and soul total connection philosophy. *Intellectual Chemistry* is where communication just flows, you can talk about anything and everything. You are able to learn from one another, share ideations about life, the world, and philosophies of living. There tends to be an understanding of respect and tolerance for one's own thoughts and feelings, even if they differ.

Most people "assume" this has much to do with IQ, though it has more to do with emotional intelligence, self-control and confidence, knowing there will be disagreements though you still love, like and respect one another.

Intellectual Chemistry does have to do with similar values and beliefs, don't get me wrong. Though, also has encompasses the concept that one can be their own person outside the relationship. There's interdependence, versus codependence.

How often have you told your partner: "I love you, though don't agree with you right now?" Or, more likely does it go calling each other names or criticizing one another? "That's stupid!" "What a dumb idea!" or "Why would you ever think such a thing; even kids are smarter than that!" "What a dumb Ass!"

Mind Chemistry is the mutual place in how you handle disagreements, struggles and challenges in similar fashions. When there is a clash in *Intellectual Chemistry,* one may be yelling, screaming or barking orders, while the other is more passive and reserved. There tends to be a great sense of winning and losing, and not being on the same page in how to work together. The "Let's work together as a team" approach is just not there.

If this is lacking, the relationship constantly builds resentment with one, or both not feeling heard or valued in their thoughts and how they feel. Boredom tends to be the precursor here, with a craving for more mental stimulation setting in.

Now the *Soulful Chemistry* stands as an interwoven breath with Intellectual Chemistry. Soulfulness has a deeper level of emotional connection that separates it from the other two Chemistries. Where *Intellectual Chemistry* involves having similar notions for handling conflict, struggles or world outlooks, *Soulful Chemistry* is that connection on how you want to be loved and the life you want to live.

No matter if you handle conflict terrifically, and are intellectually meshed, there is no fixing when one wants a kid, and the other doesn't. Another example would be where one loves affection and the other partner doesn't. You can both talk about it, respect each other's differences and points of views, though there is no "fixing" a major essence of a person's way of living or being loved. Yes, there is compromise, of course, though these are the elements of love and a relationship that are at the core of yourself.

Soulful Connection involves being on the same page on love styles, romance, expressing feelings, how you both relate in sharing compassion and empathy. Another example may be parenting. You both want two kids, though one is very permissive in parenting, and the other is extremely strict, and neither is willing to budge.

Another example could be one is very tight with financial spending, and the other is not thrifty. These elements will clash and create major complications if there is no room for compromise.

Yes, of course, I am for compromising as I have said before. Though, I am talking about being total opposites on major life and love philosophies here. At times, the yin-and-yang differences can great a harmonious balance needed in a dynamic relationship. However, when there is a full opposing perspective on the essence of a person or couple, it will be disastrous!

Even though, these three *Chemistries* are different, though do go together in having a well-balanced, healthy and connection relationship. Again, please do not mistake my words here; NOTHING is perfect! It's finding the good enough relationship where all three of the Chemistries tend to merge together between two people.

Chapter 4: Gender Stereotypes

It's the battle of the sexes! I think there was even a TV show titled as such in the 90s. Most people adhere to stereotyped propaganda as to "all men" or "all women" do such and such. Even well promoted authors write about stereotypical gender differences. I'm here to tell you that is a bunch of shit! Okay, there may be a few "accurate" ones, and I'll touch on those. However, stereotypes tend to create more distance in our society, and relationships in general. I want to create closer relationships, not further distance!

Sure, some aspects may be true. Men tend to mentally compartmentalize better than women. Another truth, may be in the way men show empathy in wanting to "fix" everything. However, we need to be aware that all stereotypes are not true. Many are born out of society's own imagination, promotions, and propagation.

Various women and men groups like to keep a separatist view. They simply feed their own biased cause. I am about fairness and equality; about sharing and being a team. It's the very myths and blatant untruths surrounding gender differences that further propel relationship problems. However, we need to start focusing on our partner's individual traits, and characteristics. We need to keep away from the mentality that has been forced fed to us over the years that *"All Men"* or *"All Women"* are the same! We must key in on what our individual partner needs to feel desired, loved, appreciated and important. Not what society deems "women" or "men" need!

Let me explain…. Often, I have couples in my office making stereotypical references: "Greg, you know how women are!" Or, *"Greg, I know you're a man, but you know how men can be!"* I actually chuckle at these remarks and simply reply: *"please tell me how women are,"* or *"go ahead; clue me in on how all of us men are."* ☺. It's at these very moments I begin teaching that they must stop focusing on stereotypes, and start focusing on what their partner needs to feel loved and desired. Stop looking at "All Women need....," or "All men want...!" Pay attention to what your lover needs as an individual, to feel adored, cherished, respected and desired!

I teach couples that perhaps certain men and certain women may exhibit love differently. However, that doesn't hold true for everyone. For example, there are women who don't like to cuddle or hold hands; while there are countless men who love and crave these things. There are men out there who are very nurturing, yet strong, and there are women who are very strong, yet cannot show empathy. You see, the main point I'm making is that you need to see your partner as an individual! Stop this: *"like all women"* or *"just like all men"* crap!

Forget about the concept that all women need this or that! Ignore the practice to conceptualize that "all men are such and such!" This causes greater disconnect and distance! Start focusing what your "Man" or "Woman" needs as an individual. We are all different and we need to propel ourselves to view life and our mates as such! Remember, there are women who love football, and men who hate it. There are also a ton of women who crave more sex than men. Go figure, right? ☺

Now take this knowledge and learn what your mate needs to feel loved, desired and important, instead of assuming and bashing either gender. After all the bullshit, we ultimately want the same thing: to be loved, desired and accepted, and to feel important as an individual!

With the numerous gender stereotypes thrown out as I noted above, there is one issue that does fall into this realm. This tends to be men's fear or backing away from confrontation with their lovers. Yes, they may be masculine, not afraid of physical altercations, however, many hate to be emotionally confronted, yelled at, feeling like a little boy getting scolded at by their parent; thus will retreat or lie. Again, I never condone these actions! I'm educating you!

Here it is Ladies, Why Men Lie to You!

This is the age-old question I get asked by my female clients and students alike. I truly believe deep down many women know the answer. Okay, maybe it's not that deep down, more like it's just below the surface. Yes, it can hurt like hell, though many women have a difficult time transitioning from getting out of their own way emotionally, allowing insecurities to control their behaviors and actions.

Now, you are reading this, stating one of two things, either: 1) *Greg, you're an asshole*, or 2) *That's right Greg, tell it!* ☺. Of course, that depends on which side of that fence you stand on. Let me throw out the extremist view: "Oh Greg is just "Mansplaining," or using "Man Speak." LOL

This has much to do with how much confidence and self-worth you hold. Yes confidence, and I'll get into that shortly.

For starters, men need to gain the balls to be honest, no matter what! Yes, no matter what your lady's reactions may spew. We need to stay strong, dig deep and be honest! Women however, need to get a grip and accept honesty. *"What the hell are you saying Greg; I can accept honesty!"* I can almost feel the tension build. Your eyes and mouth begin to snarl as you get ready to attack me verbally. 😊

Yes, the biggest reason, or one of the main reasons men lie to you is they cannot handle your defensive tactics. That's right, the way you get defensive, go tit-for-tat, start yelling and screaming at the one thing you crave from men: total honesty.

I know not all women get overly defensive with men being honest. Often women will lurch out, start bashing and ripping their man apart for being honest. So, guess what ladies? Men lie to avoid these situations. Again, I am not condoning men lying; NOT at all! I'm trying to help you and your lover be honest with one another; completely honest, even if it hurts like hell!

I see it on so many men's faces during sessions. Their fear and the "oh shit" on their faces, when I ask: "Go ahead, be honest." They want to run and hide! Not only are they ill prepared for the anger and attacks from their lady; they literally don't want to cause hurt feelings. It took me a long time to be completely honest with women for these very same reasons. Yes, me, Detroit's Love Guru, Relationship and Sex Specialist. Go figure, right? 😊. I didn't want to see their hurt, or feel like I was being bashed, attacked or ripped apart for being completely honest.

I got to the point where I gained confidence in myself, and in my own virtues where I'm going to stand up and be honest, no matter what! Now, there is a difference in being mean, rude, disrespectful, and a complete asshole in being honest! Never, ever do that!

Do not belittle, ridicule or degrade! I worked hard as hell at being honest, even knowing it would piss a lady off, or hurt her feelings. Again, this was not my intention! My intention was, and still remains to be honest. After all, that's what women desire, correct?

Ladies, I know it may hurt intensely to hear a man's honesty, and what he truly feels or thinks. I even spoke about emotional maturity in my first book: *Seize That Total Connection.* It's not easy and I do totally understand. Your insecurities and vulnerabilities are at stake. Again, I fully get you! Though, if you truly want your man to be honest with you, practice what you preach and gain the courage to hear the truth.

Think about this. If you ask your man: *"Do I please you sexually?"* and he tells you no. This is going to sting like hell. It would, and does for us men as well. Can you get to the place where you want to learn to be the best he's ever had? 😉. Can you respond with: *"Then, I'll learn to be great sexually with you?"* Not easy to respond from a place of assurance and confidence, while you are hurting and perhaps, devastated.

It takes maturity and self-confidence to hear the truth! Especially, when it's directed at the core essence of the woman you are. Again, I totally get it, and do fully understand! Men, you need to understand that your lady is learning, and growing to be okay hearing honesty. Don't give up! Be patient……

A final note for MEN! If you screw up and did something wrong, you need to man up and be honest! Yes, there will be consequences as there should be! You can't expect your lady to be all nicey-nice when you tell her you lost the rent gambling, or got caught cheating (I never, ever condone these!) You need to be man enough to take the hit and verbal outcries; though also be remorseful and take responsibility for your actions, period!

Another "crisis" situation lends itself to men not being able to "understand" women, more specifically, their wives or girlfriends. Am I right, ladies? 😊 Men can't always read minds! Got it! Let me repeat, Men can't always read minds! Men can be quite literal in a sense that was is spoken is what is taken seriously. Many men have a hard time "reading between the lines."

I teach women to talk more literal, as in being very specific on what you mean, need, or want. I know it sounds like a lot of work. "I want more time together," turns into an argument when the husband or boyfriend spends ½ hour more time in a week, and argues: "I did spend more time with you!" Well, technically, yes, he did. However, his wife wanted more like an extra 6 hours a week together. This sounds familiar right? Both people need to be more in sync with what "time" means.

Men, this is not all on the women! Hell no! Men need to take responsibility and ask: "What does extra time look like in hours, or days?" Also, men need to understand that this does not mean you set a time clock to this. Be open and more generalized, versus exact measurements. I know this can be difficult.

I did mention a few gender-related stereotypes I do buy into. Again, this does not mean that they always apply to everyone and every situation. The best thing is to ask was it meant, wanted or desired by your partner.

"Reading" one another can be taught by learning these facets about your partner, not based on assumptions. There are some couples who have been together for many years, that seem to just "get one another." How do you think they got there? They paid attention to one another and became very clear on each other's needs, personalities, characteristics, wants and needs. Plus, they simply asked one another.

Stereotypes can cause so much damage in a relationship, and created significant hurt and pain when one person does not live up to their partner's expectations of what a "Woman" or "Man" should be, want, act like or desire. These issues tend to manifest over time, thus deepening the resentment, fear and disconnect. Soon you will feel a huge disconnect and start asking yourself if your partner really loves or understand you. Remember, she/he will be doing the exact same thing.

A lack of honesty, being open and creating emotional safety just adds further distance. This can be prevented by simply asking questions and stop assuming based on predisposed stereotypical notions.

If you keep assuming, not being open, and honest and learning about your partner, you will start questioning everything in your relationship. Then, soon will be in Stage 3, unless the stereotype fallacies stop existing.

Chapter 5: Stage 3-The Storm Awakens

I want to quickly walk you through the first two stages of a relationship to give you a better understanding of the infamous stage 3. This book is set up to help you either decrease the impact stage 3 has on your relationship, or hopefully, keep the Stage 3 Storm from hitting altogether.

Many people know the feeling of falling in love as infatuation wraps its powers around us. I even spoke on this a few chapters back. We feel great as there are no flaws in one another. The endorphins kicked in and we feel high on love and so alive! I love these feelings too! Life and love are at a constant high. Being perfect together is the ambience that is never questioned! This is stage one of a relationship.

Stage 2 is the *"in true love"* realm, where both people think everything is great, little arguments or annoyances are "no big deal." There's a better sense of who your partner is, and at the same time, revealed vulnerabilities make us feel even more safe and connected. Plans of moving in together, or marriage, are swirling all around the air. This is a deeper, truer *"real love."*

You both feel comfortable with one another, farting, burping; even using the bathroom in front of each other. LOL. Things are great here in Stage 2! You are even able to handle simple disagreements or arguments with no problem. The future is filled with dreams, hopes, having kids, the house, and the family you've always dreamt about!

Now you have that house, the kids, the bills, the friends and work lives. You think you are living the dream, then a rude awakening occurs. Stress and Resentment sneaks in, and you are totally caught off guard. Those simple disagreements turn into blown out shouting matches. Expectations are forgotten, as long as knowing how your partner wants to be loved drifts away. You find yourselves so disconnected and not feeling cared about, let alone desired. These feelings become so overwhelming. We selfishly focus on our own feelings, pain, hurt, feeling not love or desired. Yet, we forget that our partner may be feeling the very same way.

A sense of "What the hell just happen," or "How did we get here, when we were so in love" slaps you. Questions if you made the right decision in a life partner start pounding at you. There are thoughts of past hurts, episodes of being disrespected, and feelings of not knowing who you are any more. Bouts of rage, sadness, and disbelief quickly follow. Welcome to Stage 3, the Storm.

Stage 3 can hit after 1 year, 5 years or even 20 years. It's different for each couple. I can attest, the possibilities are high that the storm will hit eventually. Not being pessimistic or negative, I'm trying to prepare you to work through the storm so your relationship can become stronger; you feel more in love and have a deeper appreciation for one another and your relationship.

As I noted previously, it is my hope this book helps you swerve away from Stage 3 altogether, or at the very least, limit its deadly impact.

Stage 3 is where most couples are at when they seek my help. There's been an affair, threats of divorce, sleeping in separate rooms, no touching, kissing, or connection. Most couples at this point need help to uncover the hurt, resentments or trauma created by one another, or life in general. Perhaps a very familiar saying pops up during Stage 3: "I think we just grew apart;" We're not the same people we were 10, 20 or 30 years ago."

My belief about growing apart is caused by not paying attention to one another. This involves not being aware, or making necessary adjustments to reach for another, as changes in life occur.

Another common element is when one person loses herself or her identity. For example: A stay at home mother begins to feel isolated, trapped and tied down. All of sudden, she wants to party and live life like a single person. He is "going through a mid-life crisis." More commonly, Stage 3 typically feels like you both hate one another, don't know one another, and want to get revenge for feeling hurt or pained. It's the point where you "appear" to hate one another. Words of divorce, separation, or a breakup are verbally thrown about with each breath.

There is hope and you can recover the love you once embraced. The relationship can be honest, passionate, loving and blissful and continue forever as such. This is Stage 4 *(Reignited Love)* and Stage 5 *(Peaceful Love)*. It does take work from both of you! Love can be reignited if you both desire and crave! Love, Sex & Everything In Between can help if you implement its teachings.

PART II: CONNECTING EMOTIONALLY

Chapter 6: Emotional Separation

Emotional connections are where most couples start the downward spiral. We argue, fight, or simply live as lifeless zombies sharing the same house. I can't tell you how many clients come into my office and say: *"Greg, we don't get it, we argue about the dumbest shit!"* This is where I begin teaching and provide enlightenment to flip that script on their relationship. I want couples to start *"getting it,"* so when problems surface, they can stop these tendencies before the shit hits the fan.

Most couples argue about the smallest stuff that typically is not crucial. You know why? Because they are afraid, scared or shy in discussing the deep, important and truly emotional shit. It's scary to feel, let alone express that we don't feel loved, important or desired. These feelings fester inside as we fear our partner knowing our "true" feelings: that our partner actually doesn't desire us, or hates us, or doesn't really care about us? What about finding out the truth that our lover isn't turned on by us?

Facing these possibilities leaves us in a paralyzed state. We often believe it's better *(actually safer)* hiding these fears than uncovering the painful reality. Our deepest feelings may not represent the truth, but instead of bringing it out in the open, we curl up and distance ourselves, or begin acting like an ass! Now the foundation is laid for arguments, and most of these surround the "small, unimportant shit," because we fear the deep-rooted issues. These small issues are safer to argue about, versus the deep rooted, ego-shattering possibilities. To realize that our partner actually doesn't love us, or is turned on by us is incredibly excruciating!

One or both partners often don't feel heard, cared about, desired, loved, important, you name it! What happens now is we start arguing about chores, the kids, the in-laws and outlaws. You can see where I'm going with this, right? The screaming and yelling kick in, or maybe you two are the ones who fight silently. You don't talk to one another, acting as if everything is "fine." Though, you both know its total bullshit; don't you?! The tension surmounts, you're not touching one another and feel like running and hiding. The air is filled with all this silence; even your kids feel it! I understand this very much and empathize with you! My heart and compassion go out to you! Living like this, sucks.

Back to the arguing and screaming matches. Arguing typically erupts into rants and raves followed by *"You Bitch!"* or *"You're a Fucking Asshole!"* Have you been there? These verbal lashings and derogatory names are flung with dead accuracy. They hit your inner most insecurities. See, those small things you argue about actually are protecting the pent-up, gut-wrenching feelings of not being loved, respected or desired. We can't hide or fake these feelings any more so we're forced to explode! Sound familiar? When the arguing is over, many are left wondering: "Does he really believe I'm a Bitch? Well if so, then screw whatever he wants from me; forget it!"

The most beneficial tools you need to start using are: *"I love," "I care about you,"* or *"You mean the world to mean."* Then you can follow with your issue at hand: *"though I'm mad at you!"* By verbalizing these feelings of care or love, you reduce the defensiveness and listening kicks in. This will help reduce arguing and the screaming matches. You will start to feel listened to and heard; at the same your partner will not feel attacked and more open to caring.

Most people don't realize the deeper emotions are presented by surface fights or distance. We don't want to admit our deepest vulnerabilities or so-called weaknesses. Our fears, traumas, hurts and insecurities are kept hidden. So, instead we name call, pick fights, or give each other the silent treatment. The sad thing is that these destroy emotional safety, and typically have little to do with what we are truly feeling. Instead, we blast one another and attack our loved one's insecurities. A shame, isn't it? Speak from hurt, not anger! "I felt hurt, disrespected, not loved, not desired, are examples to use. Easy, nope, though start practicing!

As mentioned at the beginning of this section, the feelings of being unimportant, unappreciated, unloved, not desired or you name it, are at the foundation of what's really happening. We can only handle so much of this hurt, then we let it out by arguing about the stupid shit! We're afraid to bring up the deep emotions and fears that are churning inside. The sooner we learn to connect to these painful roots and express them from the heart, the more connected we will feel in the relationship.

It's simply not easy to start uncovering the real emotions; though it will become second nature. The more comfortable you become in doing so, I promise you will be able to heal and feel emotionally closer to one another. Both of you will feel more understood, and that your partner *"gets you."* At this spot, you will further put your emotional walls down and actually look for the underlying hurts in the relationship, versus waiting until it gets out of control. Resentment towards one another will be decreased and walking on eggshells will cease.

Feeling unloved, or that we don't excite our partner, simply sucks and destroys our confidence and sense of self. It's scary as hell to ask our partner the deep-rooted questions, and have the answers be: *"Yes, you don't turn me on,"* or *"You're right; I don't feel in-love with you anymore."* Most of us are scared to hear the confirmation of the possible gut-wrenching feelings we hold. Thus, we keep pushing these fears deeper.

Instead, we start nagging or arguing about the unimportant shit, and this becomes the norm. This keeps circling like a vulture, waiting to devour your dying relationship.

I want to help you break the fears in asking these questions; hell, any question! Instead of pushing the real issues aside, I want you to be able to address them as soon as they pop up. If you don't feel desired, loved, appreciated or important, you can bravely share these feelings to your partner. No more hiding them. Helping couples gain confidence and breaking this fear, is a primary focus in my office. I try to get you to verbalize these "real" rooted feelings to your partner. You do this from the heart, versus the safety of screaming, yelling and anger. I help build each individual's confidence and self-worth; at the same time as instilling a loving, passionate relationship.

Chapter 7: Creating Emotional Safety

Emotional safety goes hand-in-hand with connection. Yet, many couples don't realize, or more commonly, aren't taught this. Feeling emotionally safe within the relationship is so crucial that if it's not present, the relationship starts to die. It becomes an agonizing death to say the least. The relationship's demise leaves a heavy path paved with the corpses of passion, desire, respect and love.

We start retreating our true feelings as a safeguard to protect our hearts and souls. It's no surprise that this is due to the previously mentioned domains: being fearful to express our true worries or insecurities. We fear our partners don't love us, desire us, or they simply don't care. Sound familiar as I just mentioned these?

The physical separation shortly follows as touching dwindles and kissing is just a routine peck on the cheek if at all. Sex? What the hell is sex? You start forgetting what sex, or making love feels like. The softness of each other's skin and how it feels to intertwine your souls with the physical pleasures, are far away memories.

We need to make our partners feel safe, both emotionally and physically. Sadly, many people have no clue they're not providing this safe emotional place. Comments as: "*that's stupid,*" or *"why would you feel that way,"* even, *"that's crazy you feel that way,"* all slowly kill the emotional safety. These are tame examples; believe me! In my office, couples have belittled one another with sexual ineptness, weight issues, their jobs, parenting skills, family of origins, and the list seems never ending.

As you let your imagination wander, you can come up with numerous adjectives and F-bombs, bitches, assholes, etcetera, that either start or follow up the verbal assaults. Yet, it never amazes me how many people still wonder why their love is afraid to "open up." In Chapter 6, I touched on expressing your "real" feelings as a starting point. Express from the heart, versus the fear and anger! This goes the same for listening and learning from the heart as well.

I guarantee that the above relationship practices will be a huge factor in causing love's death! Emotional safety must be guarded, protected and cherished! Many people get it's important to feel emotionally safe within a relationship, though have no clue how this is, or was initially created.

More importantly, most people don't know, nor were taught how to get the emotional safety back.

You see, those verbal rants: "*You're a fucking idiot*" or "*That's a dumb ass idea!*" or "*If you weren't such a bitch*" kills emotional safety! Duh, right! ☺

Remember, the time when you told your sister or best friend about the turmoil you are going through? That your husband is a dick, or has no clue what he's doing as a father. What about the time your wife found out you told your best friend that she's a dead fuck? These discretionary feelings need to be kept between you two! If you need help, get it! Do NOT throw each other under the bus to friends or family members! Sharing your intimate details with others, will place a wedge between you two that is difficult to remove. This "*emotional cheating*" is just as debilitating as verbally bashing your partner with the damaging comments exampled above.

As a side note: Yes, we do need a friend or close family member to vent to. This is different that bashing your partner, or spreading every single detail! Vent with trying to learn a different perspective or insights, not to belittle or degrade your partner! The only exception I teach to tell someone, is where there is a severe domestic violence incident, or chronic abuse going on. You need help, though must be smart in making plans to get out of these situations.

Okay, back on track! It shouldn't be news that these practices create a lack of emotional safety and trust in the relationship! How can you expect to be emotionally connected when you fear your partner will be blabbing the sanctity of your relationship all over the place? Yes, we need to vent to our best friend from time to time, though do NOT bash one another, or rip the very soul out from under your partner! You need to be a team and work on your issues together, or seek professional help!

Another issue I'm going to address is not following through with what you say you're going to do. This is another avenue in killing emotional safety and trust. As you are aware, if not following through is a pattern, your words mean shit. Basically, your partner will feel disrespected and begin to not trust you. Your loved one won't believe a word you say when you express: "Oh, I'll take care of such and such."

Rightfully so, you will lose respect which further festers resentment. Sooner or later, your partner will not trust what you say, and will even begin to doubt your love and dedication. Follow through on your word!

I get life happens and emergencies pop up. I'm not referring to these situations. I'm referring to the ones where there is no legitimate reason for not following through. Besides killing emotional safety and trust, your lover will not feel important.

How many times have you heard: *"I know you're physically here, but your mind is off somewhere else?"* This additionally hinders emotional connection and safety. Your partner will feel like you don't care or give a rat's ass if s/he is there, or not. Do you often get an answer that has nothing to do with the question you asked? Then you know what I'm getting at. If you're not present in your relationship, it will add to relationship disconnect and its death.

Remember, I mentioned previously about the nagging and bitching going on in your relationship? This is probably one of the biggest reasons your partner verbally attacks you. You need to make your partner feel important and that you are emotionally present in your relationship. If this doesn't take place, over time someone else will! Be present and follow through on your word..........

Not feeling important, heard or listened to all encompasses ways in how emotional safety dwindles. We often don't even realize it. Before we know it, it's too late. So, what can you do to keep emotional safety in your relationship? Stop the dumb shit that I mentioned above! This is a no brainer, right?

Seriously, this isn't a fun situation to endure, and soon to follow will be shutting down altogether. Stop this now! Should you or your partner get to the point where you no longer care about the name calling or belittling, this is a point where desensitization seeped in. You no longer care to even talk, argue or fight……Now the death of the relationship is near.

Chapter 8: Paying Attention

I want you to look and see if you're paying attention to the warning signs in your relationship. I gave a bunch of examples already regarding emotional safety and bashing episodes. Okay, are you really paying attention to your lover and relationship!? First, assess how much distance is in your relationship. Is most of the time spent *"together"* only surrounded by friends and family? Can you honestly say you spend enough time alone together; just you two?!

It's very easy to get distracted when at an event. Friends or family pull you this way or that way, soon you forget you two arrived together. Usually the guys are talking with the guys; the women with women. You two may be in the same house, or at the same event, though rarely are you *"together."* Try checking in with one another. A simple kiss, touch, or verbal gesture can mean so much! These simple, yet often forgotten acts can have a positive impact in maintaining connection and presence.

My advice is to make plans for just the two of you, and do it often! I get it *"But Greg, we get bored."* Then perhaps you need to pay attention at rebuilding your emotional connection. Remember those days when you could just sit and not do anything, yet feel so close?

Paying attention means not only being physically present, it means being emotionally there! If you often day dream when together about other things: chores, the game, your reality TV shows, pretty soon distance will manifest its ugly head. You will soon be feeling alone, left out, and not connecting on any level. Maybe your partner already feels this way. Why don't you ask?

Many couples in my office complain about this very thing. Find ways to stay engaged by touching one another, stare at one other, and kiss during commercials. We get distracted when out with others. Though, we also get distracted by our phones, tablets, TV's and the world around us. We stop paying attention to one another, then soon the lonely feelings sneak in and it becomes harder to reconnect. It forms a habit that pathetically we get used to. This shows in the form of *"not knowing what to talk about,"* or not wanting to complain or nag. Do little things to show you care and that you're emotionally present and available! Show your lover they are crucial in your everyday life! I added a few tools in the back of the book to help you with this.

Another complaint lies in the mass amounts of couples stating they "don't get one another." How can you get one another if you never, or rarely pay attention! This involves realizing their moods, if they had a bad day, excited, stressed, or you name it! Do you come home each day and greet one another? I'm not referring to the routine hug and kiss. Yes, I said routine, meaning its common practice without any feelings or thought behind it. It's programmed and robotic.

We don't pay attention many times to our lover's facial expressions. Perhaps, we are too busy or overwhelmed with life; I get it. Though, we must pay attention when we are acting like robots? But how? When was the last time you actually showed your partner you were excited to see them? When was the last time you felt that same excitement from them? Do you even care?

It is so crucial to be aware of your partner daily! Pay attention to facial expressions, moods, interests, and what's going on in their day. Not only pay attention, express that you do love them and care what is going on! For starters, begin asking questions. *"Are you having a good day?" "Are you oaky, you look a bit stressed or upset (or happy, awake, etc)?"* Simple questions show your love you care and that you are paying attention! You are being there and making your loved one feel important. Use the above suggestions and you can see your relationship become closer once again.

Remember, it's easy to fall back into old habits. Fight these! If you feel like your lover is not paying attention to you, kindly voice it. Again, speak from the heart not the anger that is burying the hurt. Asking your partner if they feel distant or not connected to you, is a great way to check in as well. By asking and noticing your partner, it shows you care about him or her, and the relationship! Start doing this today!

An added note. Yes, we need alone time! I always promote maintaining our individuality. This keeps our relationships fresh, energized and fulfilling on many levels. There must be a balance though. Have fun meeting up with your friends on occasion, doing your favorite hobby alone is good and healthy. Just make sure to make one another feel connected at the same time. *"Honey, have fun with your friends tonight; I love you"* is a simple way to stay connected. It's when this alone time becomes more prevalent and more of a priority, that these elements will cause relationship challenges. Pay Attention!

Chapter 9: Making Your Partner Feel Good About Her or His Self.

I wanted to add this important chapter. Albeit a short chapter, it doesn't reduce its significance when it comes to connection and passion in a relationship. Making your partner feel good is not what you think: "Oh yea Greg, I make my love feel really good sexually!" LOL. Okay, that is important of course, though I am referring to making your love feel appreciated emotionally.

It's very easy for many of us to pick apart the things our partner does that pisses us off, or makes us annoyed. I think we are all guilty of that; me included. How often do you recognize that good things your love does? I'm not talking about the job promotion, or opening her own business. Those are dynamic things, though I'm referring to the everyday things your love does.

Let me explain. Do you tell your love: "Wow, that was awesome how you handled the kids when they were fighting!" Or, "I'm jealous, you bust your ass at work, and still have the energy to play with the kids and make them feel loved!” It’s the little “usual” things we witness on a daily basis that we take for granted.

There are literally new events or actions that occur daily that we can acknowledge in our partner! I gave a few examples already. Additional recommendations center on the simple things your partner does. The way they handled a disgruntled relative or co-worker; to the way they make your feel supported throughout the day, or a difficult time in your life (ex: when your parent or relative had cancer and they handled the majority of life’s tasks).

Seeking out the good in your partner does not take uncovering the grandiose and exotic events. Acknowledging the simple day to day events or actions can mean the world to your love. Your love with feel appreciated and acknowledged! We don’t have to follow suit with the constant negative news reporting antics. Start looking for the good in one another and make your love aware you noticed.

Yes, a very short chapter, though one that is crucial! Think about this well researched ratio: Implement the 5:1 practice of acknowledging “5” good things your partner has done every day, to the 1 negative, you will start to witness a happier, more connected partner and relationship.

Part III: Enhancing Your Sexual Essence

Chapter 10: Sexual Fears & Insecurities

Most likely you have skipped right to this chapter to read the juicy and sensual realms. 😉. What you have read up to this point will help you dive into your sexual lives and prepare you to explore and enhance your sexuality. It takes confidence, awareness and emotional fortitude to grow to the sexual self, you desire. Not only do I hope to help you express your individual sexuality more fully, I would love that it's propelled in your relationship! So, are you ready to evolve sexually?

Ladies, be honest......how many of you would love your man to remove your panties with his teeth......oh so slowly, as his fingers gently, yet purposely caress your inner thighs. As you squirm in anticipation, you become wet as hell as his tongue follows his fingers… Then as you gasp for a breath, his mouth engulfs your pussy! He fully tastes you as his tongue caresses your lips. You are soaked and delightfully tense as he now begins to suck your clit. Are you with me ladies? ;) Would you love this?!!! Then please keep reading……

Gentlemen, would you love your lady to unfasten your pants with her teeth? Her ultimate purpose is to bring you pleasure as she begins to kiss and tease your lower stomach, then hips. She gently glides her hands across your groin, as she firmly grabs your hard cock and takes it in her mouth as a wild obsession..... Guys, does this sound hot? I'm a guy, and hell yes it sounds fucking PHENOMENAL!

How many of you are now getting squeamish or disgusted in the words used above? Or, are you giggling like a school kid? Well, stop it! Sexuality is very human and it's okay to be sexual and enjoy it! Forget about the lies and deceptive tactics used by your parent, religions, and the conservative masses to scare you away from sexual pleasures or fantasies. I'm going to help you become more aware and comforted in bringing out your sexual fantasies and cravings. Yes, we all have those and it's perfectly okay! There's nothing wrong with having and embracing these! I'm going to help you with your sexual maturity and evolution that will last a lifetime!

First, it is so crucial to note: many have endured sexual abuse or traumatic rape. This, I fully understand, and so very much empathize with every one of you! I get it, and understand how such a wonderful emotional and physical pleasure has been tainted, turned disgusting, and flipped your stomachs upside down at the very thought of sex. There have been literally countless children, teens, women, and men I have helped through these traumatic experiences. I'm here to help you as well gain back your power and control, that was once stolen from you! Yes, stolen! You didn't give that away. Got it, it was not you're doing or fault!

The above and following paragraphs are graphic, and meant to bring emotional and physical joy beyond what you could ever imagine! Most likely you are saying, "YES, I want that NOW! Well, minus me mentioning the traumatic events. This is because you deserve a healthy and tantalizing sex life that YOU control, not someone forcing you! Take my hand please as I guide you safely, purposefully, joyfully and most importantly, help you get rid of the sexual fears that have engulfed you.

Too often couples are shy or emotionally unable to talk about their sex life. Well, beyond *"we aren't having enough,"* or *"you make me feel like a piece of ass."* I'm talking about "really talk" about sex: what you desire, what you want to try, and how you want to feel. Typically, one of you is more than willing. However, the other constantly throws out comments as: *"Is all you think about is sex?"* What about: *"Our sex life is just fine, why do you always want to talk about our relationship?!"* These statements are intentional deterrents to remain comfortable and prevent sexual growth. Let's face it; many hate the thought of reaching beyond their comfort levels.

I want you to look deeply into the reasons why you are timid *(or simply scared shitless)* to openly talk about your sex life and perhaps improving it. Yes, not just the physical elements associated with porn star movements, but the emotional eye-to-eye, soul gazing connection that you can cherish. This is deep, and can reignite, plus awaken your connection on many levels. Not just the sexual!

Look now at the essence of your fears in sharing yourself with your lover. Hell, even acknowledging them with yourself. Wouldn't you love to become more emotionally and physically confident being more seductive, sultry, loving, flirtatious, or even dirty?

Addressing your insecurities is the first step in allowing this growth. This part is needed so we can address them, thus heal these fears and myths forever. I know it's scary, even panic inducing for some. I get it, and have been there myself. We all have sexual insecurities, even I do! Yes, me too!

It's okay, though instead of running and hiding, I want to be there with you as you move past these. It's my purpose to guide you in opening up your sexual self-esteem, confidence and awareness as you evolve sexually. This evolution involves not only the physical realms, it embraces the crucial emotional as well. Can you imagine bringing yours and your loved one's fantasies to life? I'm sure just thinking about it has you smiling now. Let's kick those insecurities down the damn road!

Poor body image, inexperience, not being attractive enough, not wealthy enough, hung enough, last long enough, wet enough, can't cum and the list continues to migrate an endless array of euphemisms. These create insecurities and let's face it; sex is at the essence of our pure selves. We show ourselves not only in our birthday suits, but we tend to exhibit our emotional core as well through sex.

Are you afraid to have sex with the lights on? Be completely naked, or stare into each other's eyes? These are some of the true tests involved that scare the hell out of many people-to be fully seen, body and soul. The trick is often asked: how do we get rid of these fears and paranoias?

It cracks me up when people say fake it until you make it. This philosophy may work with many other life aspects, but you can't fake sexual confidence and most people know this. Men and women both know you can't "act" through sexual and erotic comfort and expression. I'm not talking about those who are arrogant, thinking they are sexual gods or goddesses. These people are typically selfish and suck as lovers. I'm getting into those selfish, narcissistic-in-nature individuals here. Typically, "acting" creates tension, stiffness and robotic movements that your partner can feel. You know it, and s/he knows it. So stop trying to fake or act!

I'm referring to admitting your sexual insecurities, and actually owning them! "Okay, I'm not good at, or have experience doing such and such, but I want to get better!" Sounds crazy to admit these to another, though just getting them out of you frees the tension, plus you come across as humble and wanting to grow. Both of these are sexy and confidence boosters.

Gaining sexual confidence starts with being okay with your vulnerabilities. I didn't say you had to like them!

Just be aware and realize they won't be in your life forever! Remember what I said a bit ago, we all have sexual insecurities? You, me, your partner, and past lovers all have them. Having the desire to work past these is the key. The willingness to learn, become educated, and practicing will help you become more passionate, free and erotic like you've always dreamt about. I don't know anyone who rode their bike, or tied their shoes correctly on their first attempt. Relax a little, and let me show you some ways to overcome your sexual anxieties.

We tend to center on the negative within ourselves. *"I'm too fat, tits too small, not tall enough, no six pack,"* and the list ensues as we wage an attack against our own body image, and selves. We can't do many things about our bodies without being rich and undergoing painful plastic surgery. I'm not promoting those things either! We can control our eating habits and engage in an exercise routine. No, these are not fun, but… Being comfortable in our own skin is an important element in our sexual growth and essence. What would it take for you to say: *"Fuck it, this is me and I'm fine with this?"*

There will always be people attracted to us physically and willing to engage with us sexually. After all, if you currently are or have ever been in a relationship, this proves this point. I can tell you that most relationship problems I come across generate around the emotional elements, not the physical. Surprise! 😉 Look around you and you can see people, men and women who are considered obese, yet own their sexiness and others find them attractive. Their confidence shines through and that aura is what grabs others attraction.

Yes, you can improve your body image, though it does take work and discipline. Eating healthy, exercise and even stomach-related surgeries are available. Again, I am not recommending these! These are not easy strategies, and I too hate exercising, though I like the results, plus it helps immune defenses and reduces stress levels. All good things!

It does take work and discipline to instill positive growth to cement life-long changes. You will screw up and get lazy at times, just cut yourself some slack; then carry on your mission. Even finding help through resource or support groups is advised.

Remember, this is your body and you can do whatever the hell you want! If you don't like it, try to change or get to the point where you're okay with yourself.

Don't fake it! Be genuinely okay with your physical self. Should you run into others who criticize you or belittle you, they don't deserve you; got it! These people are not worth your time! Anyways, if you are honestly okay with yourself physically, then other's opinions shouldn't matter, right? 😊 I told you I can be blunt and don't sugar coat things. I am compassionate and do care very much! I want you to start being positive towards yourself!

Many people can also improve their body image through dressing a given way and grooming strategies. This doesn't have to be expensive. Thrift stores for cool clothes, craigslist and Facebook groups are awesome ways to increase your wardrobe and sexual presence. This goes for both men and women! Hell, there's even many *"For Free"* groups on these lists.

So, what the hell does all that have to do with sexual maturity and confidence? A shit load! If you are so subconscious about your body, you won't be able to let yourself go sexually, emotionally, or soulfully. I want you to like yourself on all these levels! Hell, I'm promoting that you begin to love yourself! Yes, even with our physical imperfections. The more comfortable you are in your own skin, the more you will enjoy sex, sexuality and the pleasures these provide.

Actually, people who are uncomfortable with their body image typically are submerged into pleasing. They are all about giving sexual pleasure endlessly to their partners. Fantastic and where can I find someone like this; right? 😊 The problem is, they have a hard time allowing this pleasure to be returned. It's easier to center on their partner's pleasure, while ignoring their own. Images, thoughts and feelings surface: *"I'm gross, ugly, fat, too skinny, etcetera."* Therefore, feelings of not deserving pleasure creep in." I regularly hear the all too frequent comments: *"If I don't always worry about pleasing my partner, they will leave me for someone with a bigger dick or tits, a thinner body, lasts longer, tighter pussy, or has a better ass."* Sound pretty familiar?

Another crucial element surrounding body image is self-care. I mentioned grooming above. There are countless complaints I hear from both genders that their partner *"doesn't care what they look like any more."* This is different from being confident! They continue in frustrated tones: *"Boy, when we were dating, she would look so nice, smell good, hair and make-up done, and it turned me on so much. Now, we're married (or living together) she acts like she doesn't care anymore." "He would look good, clean and put together, now always dresses like a slob."* It feels your partner, like you're saying: "I got you now, so you're no longer worth taking the time to look nice."

I'm not saying either one of you needs to get dressed up for a night on the town every day; hell no! Though, a little care can do wonders to show your lover you give a shit and they are worth looking nice for. This is definitely not just directed towards the ladies! Men, you need to keep your shit together as well! Showing you care by working on your own shit! Besides, when we tend to smell sexy and look good, if makes us feel better about ourselves. Guess what? This ultimately adds to our overall body image and self-confidence in huge positive ways!

Chapter 11: The Truth About Sexual Desire

Desire and desire discrepancies has widely confused many people and professional alike over centuries. It is one of the most talked about topics amongst friends. "My wife is never horny!" "My husband seems to always be too tired to have sex." "S/he must not be attracted to many any longer, because s/he never wants sex." I'm sure you've heard these or similar comments. Most likely, you have even said a few of your own. ☺

A key element to desire is simply pleasure. Yes, pleasure triggers desire. The more pleasurable sex is, the more desire is created. Sounds incredibly simple, right? Not necessarily so. There are numerous things that can destroy desire as you might guess. Exhaustion, lack of sleep, having young children, illnesses, depression, anxiety, fear of getting pregnant, abuse, feelings of being berated, degraded, and the ended list can continue.

I also want to add additional elements that involve desire decreasing elements. Rape, incest, emotional and sexual abuse, our own depictions of ourselves, insecurities most definitely can wreak havoc on sexual desire. These are beyond difficult to heal, though it is possible. My heart goes out to you in these situations! I have worked with countless who have endured such devastating events, and guess what, they learned that they deserve sexual pleasure too. Now on their terms, not the fucker's who abuse them.

Increasing desire needs to begin with wanting. Do you want more sex in your life and relationship? What is sex to you? I talk about the mind, body, heart and soul of a relationship and sex throughout this book. Have you deciphered what sex is to you? Who taught you about sex? Are there myths that you follow, like "sex is something you need to do if you're a wife, or a woman." Or, "sex ends once your married, or at a certain age?"

What are your beliefs about sex, about the pleasures you'd like to receive from sex? Are you able to discuss these questions openly and honestly?

Sexual desire is about pleasure, though it's more than the physical pleasures derived. What are the emotional, mental and soulful pleasures you want to experience from sex? Most want to feel loved, appreciated, cherished along with the physical enjoyment. The next few chapters will guide you in exploring the questions I asked above. If you don't have the answers to these questions, that's perfectly okay. Don't fret. You can always find your answers later.

Remember this important tip: Sexuality, sexual pleasure, your thoughts and views on sex are yours. No one else lives your life! You do not need permission to enjoy sex the way to you desire! Well, it does need to be consensual amongst the people involved. 😊 Sex is not based on what your parents' views are, what religions dictate, what your friends or professionals decide for you. Sex is based on what you value, enjoy, desire and decide!

Chapter 12: Sexual Syllabus

My sexual syllabus is to teach you the elements involved in a dynamic sexual relationship; my classroom course criteria if you will. I am not here to pressure you or place demands on you. My intent is to help you learn in becoming the dynamic lover you desire! Plus, I bet your partner will love it too!

I spoke about insecurities before and these can be explored in conjunction with the sexual syllabus criteria. Please relax, remember no pressure and learning is to be fun. You don't need to place unrealistic porn star expectations on yourself! So here are the classroom content areas in no primary order:

1) Emotional Connection
2) Kissing
3) Fore-Play
4) Verbal Expression & Guiding
5) Oral Sex Pleasing
6) Freakiness/Openness to Exploration
7) Physical Pleasure
8) After Glow Care

Chapter 13: Emotional Seduction

A huge emotional component that gets neglected over time is seduction. Seduction enhances your sexual relationship and increases the love juices between you two. It makes your partner feel craved, wanted, desired and loved. Get it? These are all emotional longings. An emotional-sexual connection is the foundation to a wonderful, soulful and exhilarating sex life! This is why I placed the emotional connection first on my sexual syllabus. It catapults the emotional longings we crave at the most primitive levels.

Remember long ago, how you would stare at one another, and literally taste your lover's lips before even kissing? What about how you were sultry in your posture, your gestures, and longings with your soulful eyes. Where did those feelings and emotional fires go? You can get them back, plus learn to never let those slip away again! Seductive actions trigger the emotional longing and bring about the warm stirrings that we are afraid to admit, have escaped.

Crucial: it's each other's responsibility to bring seduction back into the relationship! It's not just the *"man's"* or the *"woman's"* job; it's both of yours! Would you like to reignite eroticism and the passionate juices again? Oh, wait, let me guess; the "but" and "however" get in the way..... No time, the kids, work, family, you name, are just some of the *"but's"* and *"however,"* we need to eliminate. I will help you get rid of excuses, fears and insecurities, while allowing your inhibitions to slip away. Tell me, would you love that? Now, let's step through some of these excuses that often get thrown at me in my office.

"Greg, how can we be that way again with our kids around?" "We need to be responsible and careful because we have kids now." I have heard so many excuses for couples losing their sexual cravings for one another. From being exhausted, pissed off, feeling taken for granted and not turning your partner on; to not feeling connected and fearful of being rejected; and of course, having kids. These *"reasons,"* albeit legit at times, start killing the emotional connection we share. We stop flirting, eye-fucking one another and touching. A huge disconnect is created, perhaps has been for a long time. We pretend sex or craving one another is not important any longer. Wanting

to devour one another sexually ceases, and the emotional death of the relationship soon follows. Sound familiar?

As I mentioned, the reasons may be legit at times. However, you both need to push through these struggles and refocus on you two! Start getting back to keeping the sexual magic alive and kicking! This begins with reigniting the emotional seducing again!

Remember those insecurities I mentioned before: being rejected by your seductive advances, or body image contemplations? Perhaps it's easier to rationalize these fears, versus fighting for your sexual identity, desires and pleasures? Actually, this whole situation is quite sad… giving up your sexuality, your pleasures, plus not making your partner feel craved.

"It's been so long, what if s/he doesn't want me to be touched, kissed or ravished any longer." Is safer to believe: "It's normal for relationships and marriages to be like this after a while." We literally start bullshitting ourselves, and buying into the myth that states we need to be okay with a lack of sexual passion and emotional fire. Don't ever be okay with that!

When was the last time you tried to turn your partner on or seduce him or her? Maybe you just don't care anymore, or perhaps it's easier than facing your fears of rejection or insecurities that encompass your every thought…. When you stop making your partner feel sexually attractive and emotionally desired, the relationship will begin to fade and become stoic. Either couples will learn to live with this, or the relationship will end. To me, both of these situations suck ass and are not conducive to happiness.

Chapter 14: Seduction is Purposeful

Seduction is purposeful and it's intended, even if it's in a teasing manner. Seduction mixed with love and lust creates a bond in its deepest and primitive form on both physical and emotional levels. It adds to the abundance of one's soul. Next, I will interweave sensuality into this delightful purpose of sexual pleasure and emotional engulfment.

SEDUCTION, hmmm are your minds wandering? So many women have thoughts of being romantically and soulfully caressed. What about being devoured in an animal-like passion, getting your clothes ripped off and being pushed up against the wall and fucked hard!? You often day dream about being swept away in breath, body and soul. Are you craving these very acts? Imagining you engulfing the intense pleasure that causes you to explode in delight?! 😉

I want to know what you're feeling now as you ponder these thoughts. What emotions are firing inside you at this moment? Are you starting to get aroused and emotionally craving these pleasures? When was the last time you've felt such intensities? When was the time your partner felt this way?

Wait ladies, what have you been doing to seduce your man? Do you rip his clothes off with that same animal-like intensity, that you desire him to do? How often have you craved this passion, though have not expressed a word about it? You'd love him to devour you like this, right? Are YOU showing him that you want to devour him as well? If not, what's holding you back? ;) Don't tell me that it's *"man's job!"* Most of us men crave these very things from the woman we love. In fact, we find it fucking hot!

Are your fears of being rejected getting ion the way of acting out these passions? I know, I ask so many questions, though, they are crucial in helping you explore your wishes and desires; your partner's too.

I promote stepping away from stereotypical gender roles. Women have the right and "should" be able to go after men that grab their interest. This applies even more so in long-term relationships. Both men and women have the power to seduce and act upon these feelings. Being seduce is not just for men to practice! Women need to be seductive and engage their sexual assertiveness as well. It doesn't make women "sluts" who act on their sexual desires and cravings! There should never be any "slut shaming," period!

SEDUCTION is not just physical. It's also a highly emotional act as well. Seduction promotes confidence and being "okay" having desires and not shying away from them. It's allowing your intentions to be seen in your eyes, soul and in the way you carry yourself in the moment.

Can you use those come-hither eyes, or apply verbal descriptions of what you're going to do to him or her? Are you too shy? Hmmm, evolving sexually is very healthy and enlightening; even delicious as hell! Remember, I spoke about your fears and trying to fight through these. I often hear: *"Why be seductive when I don't feel emotionally connected?"* This absolutely makes sense and it's hard to feel sexual when you're not connected. This is especially true if you're in a long-term relationship.

Perhaps you're not emotionally connected because the seductions have ceased. When we don't feel desired, craved, respected or valued, an emotional distance embarks. This definitely isn't a secret. What follows at this point is we shut down both emotionally and physically. We stop making one another feel craved. After all, why try seducing what can't be seduced; right? The nice gestures, compliments and attention all get flushed down the proverbial toilet. It's no wonder that we feel like shit when we feel disconnected. These are the emotional seduction strategies that are often forgotten, or taken for granted. Soon, feeling dead in a relationship, and related problems peak their heads out form hiding.

A huge part of seduction involves flirting. Let's be real, this most likely was the very first thing we did get attraction flowing between one another. We need to grab that person's attention first, right? Then the relationship developed from that point.

Flirting then starts to dwindle over time. We neglect it, take it for granted and perhaps even feels like it's not needed any longer. Maybe it's out of pure laziness, being busy, or taking each other for granted? However, you need to bring it back into your love life to reignite the passion and love! It needs to be brought back to life, using intent and purpose!

Many of the seductive forms I noted above can be seen as flirtatious acts. Though, flirting is more of a subtle approach than aggressively ripping each other's clothes off.

Batting your eyes, winking, a simple touch on the arm or cheek all represent these “light” seductive maneuvers.

Flirting tends to be more playful in nature, thus making it fun and like child’s play that brings out the little girl or boy in each of us. There’s a fun, teasing aspect to flirting that makes one another feel safe, while reduces one’s guard. Let’s face it, it’s just a cool way of telling your lover you care and are interested. Little pillow fights, water fights, little tricks are all fun ways of bringing back the love and passion in your relationship. Just make sure the tricks aren’t death, or serious injury causing! LOL

Besides the fun gestures as grabbing each other’s booties, flirting can be romantic and loving in nature. The deep eye gazes, loving touches, plus little notes expressing your love, are flirtatious behaviors you can bring back into your relationship. When was the last time you actually flirted with your partner? Remember how good it felt? How much of this kind of fun and laughter was experienced way back when? Remember, how you both felt ignited, turned-on and ready to devour one another? Start doing these again and watch your stress levels decrease and closeness return.

Emotional seduction helps trigger the physical cravings. Not only do we need the physical seductive acts of touching, kissing, and caressing, we need to keep the emotional elements firing! The verbal compliments, affirmations, and being emotionally *"there"* are all crucial elements involved in seducing our lovers. Ultimately, these will bring back the emotional connections needed to reignite the sexual chemistry you and your lover crave!

Chapter 15: The Lost Art of Kissing

As the months, years, and perhaps decades pass, it amazes me how deep, passionate and soulful kissing becomes nonexistent for many couples. This is so sad and yet at the same time, people try to *"be okay"* without it. We should never be okay with just a "routine kiss on the cheek?"

How often do you actually feel one another's heart throbbing and soul in your lover's kiss? I bet it's not as often as it used to be. Perhaps as with the loss of emotional seduction, we get preoccupied with life, the kids, and work; thus, we're too tired or unmotivated. We often ignore the soulfulness and depth that passionate kissing creates. Maybe we just forgot how much we use to crave it. Perhaps we don't want to think about it, because it brings back the actual pain of missing it. We just give a kiss on the cheek like grandma would give us…a gross thought, right? Well, start changing this now!

When was the last time your tongues danced together, or that you deliciously nibbled on your lover's lips; perhaps had yours lightly bitten in ecstasy? Okay, perhaps it was the last time you made love or fucked one another. I do get that aspect, and love that myself! Though as the years pass, has kissing been left out of sex too? It's very sad, if it has….

What caused you to ignore the importance and emotional engulfment that kissing allows? Perhaps you no longer want to feel the deep connection that kissing brings, or maybe you both are just lazy? I'm not only talking about kissing during sex! When was the last time you grabbed your lover and kissed him or her so passionately that you felt them melt? Don't just wait for sex to kiss one another deeply! Do it daily and often!

As I challenge you to kiss one another deeply and passionately, and do it often; I'd like to you add a little twist. Have you ever kissed deeply while gazing into each other's eyes? Creepy, right? LOL. It's mesmerizing, soulful and encompasses that deep connection that looking into one another's eyes during sex brings. What, let me guess, you don't do that either? Well, I'll touch on that in a little bit.

Most people feel awkward or unnatural in trying this for the first time. After all, when we had our first "real" kiss, and many after, we automatically close our eyes, right? It's like a reflex: mouth opens, eyes close.

LOL. Give it a try! You may start laughing at first because it will feel awkward; so what! Do it anyways, and allow yourselves to laugh and joke, then try again. The more you relax and engulf this act I promise you it'll heighten the passion and soulful bond between you two.

Chapter 16: Fore-Play Splendors

We have all heard the importance of foreplay. Well, we should have, at least. From the onset of our sexual adventures, women have expressed a deep craving for fore-play. Yet, I still get numerous complaints about the lack of foreplay women don't receive. Guess what, Men have also complained it's lacking as well! Go figure, right? I thought men just wanted to stick it in and blow it? ☺

Over the years, foreplay has been talked about, written about, researched and perhaps become so widely rampant that is has become a boring topic. However, I am still covering it here. It never should be a boring topic! Not only does it play a crucial role in my *sexual syllabus*, fore-play creates craving, longing, enticement, and love all rolled together!

Fore-play should have meaning and depth! What meaning do you give fore-play in your relationship? Is it just about the physical pleasure? This is where you need to start educating yourself in what you desire and what oyu don't like during fore-play. It's also crucial to get this same information from your partner as well. Each of you need to start exploring not only the physical pleasures it brings, but the emotional and spiritual realms fore-play encompasses. The meaning of fore-play is an important domain in your relationship on many levels. I'm sure many of you have not explored these elements. Let's Start now…..

Yes, we all like the animalistic "*throw you up against the wall, and fuck the hell out of you*" moments. Though, most of the time both men and women like the seductive teasing and pleasure-building that foreplay produces. It enhances both the emotional and physical connections, plus entices further pleasures to come. Foreplay means you care enough to take your time in bringing out the tantalizing, teasing sensations craved by your partner.

Yes, men are included in this craving. Sadly, there still are many men and women included in the group of *"rushing"* to the finish line or "let's just *get it over.*" Other than the quick ravishing of one another (which are awesome at times!) the rushing simply builds resentment, makes your partner feel undesired, like a piece of meat, or that you are only giving a pity fuck. No one wants any of those!

What does foreplay mean to you? Grab her crotch and that's foreplay? I sure hope that's not your idea of it! Like every other relationship and sexual domain, foreplay is quite subjective and specific to each partner. Some like to be tickled and teased for an hour, while others can't stand to be *"tortured"* longer than 2 minutes. Each person is different and you need to find out what turns your partner on physically and emotionally! Yes, emotional foreplay is just as crucial!

Let's discuss the least obvious: emotional foreplay. This can entail sexting and seductive emails describing what you'd love to do to your partner. For example: *"I want to suck your hard cock until you cum!"* or, *"I want to lick you until you are so wet and squirming in ecstasy!"* These gestures get your emotions churning and desires kicking! The imagination of foreplay expressiveness tends to drive both women and men wild! It's awesome to feel craved emotionally and physically! Plus, these actions build anticipation and further craving for your partner and yourself! The emotional and feeling aspects of fore-play start churning and building that passionate fire of anticipation.

Not only expressing what you'd like to do physically and sexually, emotional foreplay should involve the subtle, loving and romantic actions. Notice the above, blunt sexual innuendoes. Now compare these to: *"I love and cherish you so much!"* or *"I love tasting your soul in your kiss and so can't wait to kiss you tonight!" "I love seeing all of you and staring into your soulful eyes when we make love; I always long for that with you!"* Do you notice the difference? The romantic, love filled expressions, versus the animalistic and raw. Both are fantastic ways to apply emotional foreplay. It's best to use both, mixing them up to entice your partner on many emotional levels: naughty-animalistic, as well as loving, adoring and soulful.

Emotional foreplay can be done by placing notes in lunches, on bathroom mirrors, on pillows and on the seat of your partner's car. Even Google ideas online!

Complimenting your partner is also a form of emotional fore-play that does wonders for one's psyche. Hit on their attractiveness to you, their intelligence, sexiness, kindness, hotness, sweetness. "You are so fucking hot to me! You can even throw in a little verbal dirty fore-play: "I love how *"nasty" you are in bed!"* 😉 The crucial thing is to be genuine, real and honest! Don't just say anything that you don't mean or feel! Your partner typically will sense when you're bullshitting.

Complimenting your lover builds closeness and is definitely a form of emotional foreplay. Thus, any written or verbal expression that tells your partner s/he is desired, loved, cherished, important or sexy, creates a deeper emotional bond. It's not just for the sole purpose of getting laid! Again, you must be honest and genuine! Don't just make shit up to sound good!

I can assure that if you don't start placing an emphasis on emotional foreplay, your lover will feel cheated, like a piece of ass, and used. Ultimately, there will be emotional separation and the demise of the relationship will set in.

Regarding men: ladies, if don't share these elements as well, they will feel like you are just going through the motions; perhaps just *"doing your duty"* or *"getting it over with."* Men like to be emotionally turned on and made to feel loved and sexy as well!

Chapter 17: Verbal Expressions

"Fuck me hard," "Suck my cock," "Lick my pussy!" are verbal expressions we love to hear or say in the heat of passion! Well, maybe it's just me! Are you offended by these terms, or find them appalling? My question is why are they disturbing to you? Perhaps it's your religious upbringing or that your prudish guardians told you: *"good people don't talk like that!"* or *"only whores use those words!"* It's sad that you were taught these myths. Yes, Myths! These lessons weren't correct and are simply contrived social control mechanisms. It'd be funny to learn those very people who taught you these words are disgusting, actually used them, themselves! It's not wrong to verbalize your sexual cravings and desires, especially in the context of a hot, loving relationship!

We tend to be sexually shy or afraid to be verbally explicit with our lover. However, when we get in heated arguments, we have no problem throwing out names like *"bitch and asshole"* like they're second nature. Kind of ironic, isn't it? Yet, we have a difficult time verbally expressing ourselves sexually? I want you to get rid of these hang-ups and misinformed negative labels you grew up to be shamed. Please remember, this is not shameful behavior and it's perfectly okay to incorporate *"dirty words"* into your sex life!

Sexual expressions, of course, also includes being comfortable verbalizing your needs, wants and pleasures! I still get many couples in my office who are timid in verbalizing what they sexually desire to one another. It may be easy to tell your partner she is beautiful, sexy, or how much you love him. However, telling your man you want him to *"lick me,"* sadly leaves many ladies queasy. It's that battle between our animalistic tendencies and the *"good girl or boy"* labels we try to portray. Get this: you are still that *"good girl or boy"* even if you use these *"dirty and nasty"* carnal expressions. There is something freeing and liberating in using our uninhabited voices. This is all part of showing ourselves fully to our lovers, as well as to our own self.

Another entity of verbal expression involves telling our partner what we love or don't enjoy sexually. This goes for the emotional realms as well. Again, we may be afraid to offend or hurt his or her feelings, so we hold back and keep it buried. I remember one couple I saw years ago….. They were married for 26 years. She became upset in the first session and blurted out: *"You haven't pleased sexually me in 20 years!"* Her husband was mortified and I even felt like I got kicked in the nuts after her proclamation. I immediately empathized with both of them, while asking her what stopped her from teaching him what pleased her? Her defensive attitude was rude and blunt: *"He's the man; he should just know, Greg!"* The root of this sad encounter was her fear of hurting his feelings and emasculating him; mixed with her own insecurities of sexual expression. Well, those went out the window during that session. For twenty years, she kept this building up and was scared to verbalize, and take ownership of her own sexuality.

This couple made huge strides in sexually expressing their needs emotionally, physically and verbally. I don't want you to take twenty years to learn the importance of verbalizing your inner most sexual desires and pleasures. Can you tell your lover what brings you pleasure: *"Damn, I love how you suck my hard cock!"* or *"You make my pussy quiver when you lick me!"* What would it take to show the very essence of who you are sexually? Let's face it, even hearing how we make our lover feel tremendous, builds our ego and turns us on even more! This "should" be a mutually shared experience!

I'm also a huge advocate of physically guiding your lover while verbalizing your desires. You can take her hand while you tell her: *"I love it when you grab my cock like this"* as you place her hand on your "manhood" using the pressure you love; or *"Touch my clit like this"* as you guide his fingers over your throbbing clit. You can definitely use physical guidance with your words to express your desires and needs. In fact, I promote it! ;)

I think the hardest may be expressing what we don't enjoy sexually; instead, we sell ourselves out and endure the suffering. This is unfortunate and needs to stop! Again, we don't want to hurt or disappoint our lover. So, we just go through the motions; not saying a word. Ultimately, we close off our own sexuality and sense of self. PLEASE stop this now!

Instead of voicing our dislikes we push sex away, thus pushing our partners away emotionally as well. There's a sense of distance and disconnect that creeps in. It's unfortunate that we hide ourselves and our dislikes. This isn't fair to us, or to our partners. I'm all about pleasing and making my lover feel incredible! I want to know what she doesn't enjoy, or makes her feel uncomfortable. Don't you want that from your lover too? I also want to be able to verbalize my displeasures. Please, don't ever hide this knowledge from your lover! You wouldn't want them to hide it from you! Both of you deserve to have your sexual desires and dislikes shared between one another other.

It takes confidence and self-insight to verbally express our dislikes, as well as our passions. There is a huge discomfort that creates an unwillingness to be open in voicing our displeasures. Remember, these are not a right or wrong. It's about learning what you both love, crave, and as well, what you dislike. Expressing these helps you both grow and learn more respect for one another and your relationship.

Verbal sexual expression is teaching our partners more about us. It can be primitive and soulful all at the same time! View these expressions as another path in furthering your sexual selves, plus your relationship.

Remember I noted about verbalizing both compliments and appreciation as part of foreplay? This will help you continue the foreplay pleasures you and your partner crave. Verbally expressing our sexual desires pulls us closer together and allows for greater self-acceptance. Don't be ashamed to verbalize your sexual self!

Chapter 18: Oral Pleasure

This lesson on oral sex is not to be an all-encompassing manual. It's just to teach you some tips and insights. I covered some graphic verbal expressions in the previous chapters and some of those encompassed oral sex. Which words of expressions sound more appropriate to you; the Loving or Nasty words? Does it depend on if you're in a loving mood, or one that screams "Rip my clothes off NOW!? 😉

No matter which mood you're in, oral sex can enhance your sexual connection in a major way. I'm sure most of you are reading this saying: *"No shit, Greg!"* LOL. I get it, though many people, men and women alike, view oral sex as giving up power to their partner. This is so not true!

This is a myth that often gets portrayed by the same mentality that verbally expressing your "nasty and dirty" sexual needs has had. Some people use unhealthy biases: *"that it's wrong, nasty and only whores, prostitutes or man-sluts do those things."* This is one of the most naïve or immature beliefs out there!

Some people still hold beliefs that oral sex is evil or nasty. However, the fact still remains that most people do enjoy oral sex and crave it in their relationship. In fact, giving oral sex places the power in your hands (or mouth). Realize that you have the power to provide great pleasure! So embrace this fact: **"By giving oral pleasure, you have the power to please!"** It's not the other way around! The receiver doesn't have the power. This of course, isn't referring to physically or emotionally abusive situations! I never, ever condone abuse in any form, nor should you!

Are there right and wrong ways of giving oral sex? Again, I'm hearing the comments pour in: *"Greg, that's nuts and crazy! As long as I get it, that's great!"* Those experienced lovers know there are difference in pleasing and being pleased orally. They get where I'm coming from, no pun intended. Not many women want to be licked like it's coming from a slobbery Saint Bernard. Yes, giving great "head" or "licking her right" is subjective like sex and life in general.

Some like it slow and gentle, and some like it fast and rougher. The intensity also depends on level of arousal being experience by the recipient. As long as it is pleasurable, or even better, down right toe curling for your lover, it's good. Keep reading as I entice you with some tips that can enhance your oral skills. I'll touch on helpful techniques later on.

Oral pleasing typically centers on the genitals, right? What if you can entice and build up the pleasure before even licking or sucking your lover's genitals? Yes, a huge part of sexual foreplay can and should involve oral teasing, tickling and pleasing. It brings one's skin alive and awakens both the physical and emotional cravings at the deepest levels.

Do you kiss or lightly lick your partner's neck or ears? What about her collarbone or inside of his arms? These are only some aspects of orally pleasuring your partner, and yes kissing and nibbling your lover's lips are included.

Before you contemplate engulfing your lover's genitals orally, do you build the anticipation by kissing, sucking, and licking your partner's nipples (yes, your man's too) or breasts? *"Greg, of course, that's a no-brainer,"* but what about running your tongue down the sides of your lover's ribs, stomach, or the crease where the legs meet the abdomen? Would you like these very things done to you? Orally pleasing "should" not just center on the genitals!

It involves the entire body as if you are caressing your partner's soul with your mouth, lips and tongue. Now, the trick is to match your oral pleasing to what your lover enjoys. She may like something totally different than what you crave. Pay attention to your partner's moans and groans in delight. This is also where your partner "*should*" verbally express his or her pleasures, likes, and dislikes.

Be wise and knowledgeable with the fact, that if you automatically dive in and start nibbling or sucking hard on your lover's nipples before they are erect, it could hurt like hell! Let your lover guide you verbally, or physically with their hand or verbal commands. Intensity, especially in women, is a slow burn, versus a microwave!

By providing directives for firmer pressure, nibbling, or tugging in the way they desire at a given time, only enhances a great orally pleasing experience!

You will be able to learn your partner's nonverbal body cues as your awareness builds. As you become one with your partner orally, chances are you won't need any verbal commands. Their body language will tell all. 😉

That doesn't mean verbal expressions can't be implemented. Most people, including me, love it when our partner verbally expresses: *"Oh god, yes, yes!"*

Remember, each person is different in how they want to be orally enticed. Learn if he likes certain body regions nibbled, while he loves others kissed or sucked. This goes along with what pressure to apply, along with when and where. Plus, what is preferred: your lips, mouth, tongue, or teeth being used as the pleasure device.

Have you ever sucked on your lover's toes, caressed the back of her thighs with your tongue? What about even kissed or licked his ass? Let's go further and ask if your partner loves her anus licked or kissed? "Disgusting!" you're yelling now! LOL

There are numerous avenues in bringing oral pleasure to your partner. What is tolerable, enjoyable and off the table, is subjective and a matter of preference to each person and couple. So, what's stopping you from, at least, trying some new oral ventures?

The thoughts of taboo, being grossed out, the taste, even germs can play a role on your oral appetite. I'm all about hygiene and this is crucial in making your lover feel more at ease, clean and even tasty.

Some people are now disgusted at my mention of a rim job, or AKA: licking your lover's butthole. People think about what body functions occur, then get squeamish in regards to orally pleasuring these spots. I do get it! As I mentioned, we all have our own sexual taboos and angsts. These need to be respected, and boundaries need to be discussed.

What if you actually enjoyed being orally pleased like this? Would that scare you more than just the thought of attempting these *"taboo"* acts? "There is no way I'm going to stick my mouth or tongue there!" "Hell no, you aren't going to kiss or lick me there!" I think people may actually be more worried about the thought of liking something *"gross or disgusting,"* versus the actual act. After all, if you'd like your ass being kissed or licked, would that make you a *"bad girl or boy?"* Would it make you a disgusting pervert? No! It would not! Not at all! It makes you very human and not deranged at all.

A first step towards easing into sucking your lover's toes or bootie hole is to make sure they are cleaned. Now that's a no-brainer! Perhaps some flavoring would help the cause in making it more appealing. If you do use flavor syrups or elements, M**ake Sure These are Sexually and Physically SAFE!** Butterscotch, chocolate, strawberry… …what's your favorite?

I want you to address your fears and ask what scares you about *"unusual"* oral acts. It's okay to have these fears, but I want you to be able to openly express these to your lover. Notice, I haven't even touched on the genitals yet. Oral pleasing means more than genital stimulation. I'm a true believer that it should be incorporated into both, fore and after-play.

Are you ready to dive into pleasing your lover orally? Longing to taste her sweet juices on your lips and tongue? Ladies, do you absolutely love it when you have your lover's hard cock throbbing in your mouth? Are you getting excited? Men, what about you; do you love how your lover tastes, squirms and how wet she gets when you lick and suck on that *right* spot? 😉

I still get bewildered at how often I hear people snarl: *"I'm not going down!"* or *"I'll never give head!"* Not only do these statements raise my eyebrows, what follows is even more confusing or perhaps annoying. I'll ask if they enjoy getting oral: "Oh sure, I love it when she gives me head!" or "Of course I love it when he licks me!" I'm like WHAT? You love getting sucked and licked, but you won't give it? You're kidding, right? Sadly, there are some out there, who aren't joking and want it a one-way street. Would you tolerate that? I wouldn't, but that's my own personal take. This is totally up to you, if you choose to tolerate this one-way pleasure street.

I understand the taboos about the rim jobs or orally pleasing your lover's ass, though what's with direct oral to genital pleasing? Especially when you love it done to you! Is this a double standard, a case of hypocrisy, or just down-right rude and selfish? LOL. I'm not being biased or judgmental! This is my own personal preference: *I will never be with a woman who doesn't enjoy giving me head. Yes, enjoys it! She doesn't just tolerate it, or feels she has too; but loves pleasing orally! The same goes for her loving me to taste and please her orally.*

Okay, enough about me… What hang ups do either gender have about orally pleasing? It could be the taste, odors, textures, or even "what comes out of there, or they pee from there." With the anal licking, I do get that dynamic. I also think that most of the issues are more generational taboos. In fact, many teens openly practice oral sex on each other. Now, I don't readily promote these teenager's acts. I'm just informing you. Yes, you parents out there may be shocked and dismayed.

With oral sex, as with any other sexual act, we can have our boundaries and limitation in what we will, or won't do. There's nothing wrong with that! I know you were waiting for this part.

However, would reducing your boundaries create a deeper sexual experience for you and your partner, plus create an increased emotional connection? Perhaps reducing your self-induced limitations would do both.

I'm going to dive right into the famous taboos associated with oral sex. The first of course is the man "coming" in his lover's mouth. The second may be with a man's leeriness of licking his lady "because she bleeds there." There are many women out there that won't allow her man "blowing it" in her mouth. I am NOT saying she has to be okay with this; I'm just trying to expand your horizons. I often hear that some women don't like the taste, texture, or just the idea of swallowing. The taste or its texture might gross some women out, while many are okay with it, or in fact, love it. Some even express that "come" is an "acquired" taste.

I am going to get rid of one myth: there is no physical harm in swallowing; unless of course there is an STD, STI, or other bacterial or viral infection. This goes the same for men performing oral on their lady. Now, let's expand on oral sex.

Chapter 19: Oral Lessons for the Ladies

First ladies, if trying to swallow or spit after your man comes appeals to you, pay attention. Why do men like coming in your mouth? You need to ask him! Every man is different and it could be the feeling of letting go of inhibitions, not holding back, or the release it provides. He may also think it's just cool, makes him feel more special that you enjoy it, or gets a great high while you tell him: *"cum in my mouth!"* Like many sexual domains, the answer is subjective and individualized.

A word of advice to ladies wanting to try to swallow for the first time: have him taste his own ejaculate before you attempt swallowing. I'm a man and this isn't wrong, homosexual, or unmanly. Ladies, you would also be wise to try a taste, and experience the texture before he completely "unloads" in your mouth.

Men will be reading this part and saying: *"What the hell is Greg saying? I thought he was a man, and he's ruining it for us!"* 😊. I'm very much a man, though I'm trying to help men and women alike. Plus, this likely will help her be more willing to "fully" please you orally. Get it?!

An added complaint I often hear from women in, and outside my office is: *"My guy will never kiss me after I suck him off; what's with that Greg?"* I agree! Men should be more than willing to kiss you right after! This keeps the emotional connection thriving and the pleasure juices flowing. Men, start doing this! Grow the hell up!

Okay, back to the ladies. I noted before in using sexually safe flavorings for oral sex. For your first attempt at swallowing or spitting for that matter, try using the many edible, flavored gels or syrups. Hell, even if you want to use these each time you please him orally! Allow yourself to get caught up in the moment, and by freely letting go allows you to fully engulf the experience. Breathing through your nose is definitely recommended as well!

Do I take it for granted that many women reading this, already practices oral sex? No, I do not! This goes with whether, or not, you "finish" the job? It's also important to know that you don't need to swallow every time. If your man demands this, then he's a selfish prick, period!

Use oral sex as a form of fore-play, even as sexual teasing. This will also drive him crazy, as your sexual anticipation builds inside your hot, steamy, wet and delicious self. 😉. You can also try finishing him off orally after you've *gotten off,* adding a more sexually charged finish.

Ladies, would you like to get better at giving head, orally pleasing and teasing your lover? I hope you are answering with an excited "Hell to the yes!" I already touched on ways to please using your mouth and tongue during the foreplay section, so now I'll center on the genitals.

Most guys love getting sucked and licked; this is another no-brainer! Here are some short tips to increase your oral talents. Again, it's important to note that each man is different, thus may enjoy different acts while receiving oral sex.

1) Most men love their balls licked and sucked; touched while getting their cock pleased.

2) The tip of the cock is the most sensitive, primarily the underneath; the bottom of the shaft is a close second, so pay attention to that area as well.

3) Nibbling is enjoyable by most, so a variety of licking, nibbling and sucking is great!

4) Use a suction action while performing oral sex; like sucking on a straw.

5) A variety of the above, mixed together with varying pressures is very enjoyable.

6) Ask your man what he loves, craves and what feels best to him.

The above mentioned is a short list of techniques that most men love, plus noting the target areas for the most pleasure. Actually, there are many guys who like their anus gently fingered too, as you're pleasing him orally.

"As long as it's in her mouth, she's good at it," is not true! Learn, ask and get excited about providing your guy with amazing oral sexual experiences! There is a book I recommend as well, that can aid in furthering your oral talents: *He Comes Next*. Remember, the power is with the giver; not the receiver!

Chapter 20: Oral Insights for Men

Men, you need to learn about pleasing your woman orally and being able to drive her wild into ecstasy, as she squirms on your tongue and mouth! I still receive many complaints from ladies who report that her man, or past exes weren't good at pleasing them orally. Licking of course is a generic term often associated with oral sex performed on a lady. Actually, that's just one technique. The how to, where, pressure and speeds are crucial to pleasing your lady. As with orally pleasing men, the "techniques" are subjective, and vary woman to woman. You need to learn what your lady enjoys, and drives her freaking wild!

A very crucial element in pleasing your lady sexually, is to make her cum first! Yes, many women are multiple orgasmic, thus allowing her to cum first, makes you more of a sexual stud. Plus, this shows you actually give a shit about her sexual needs and desires.

I spoke about taboos earlier and men's potential issues about going down. *"They bleed from there"* tends to be the most common, along with other so-called cleanliness myths. Men, you too can ease into oral sex by first taste testing to get accustomed to her flavor and scent. Use your fingers to obtain small tastes of your lover's vjj *(aka: vagina)*. Every woman is different and varies depending on if they smoke, their diet; if they are totally shaven, or fully natural.

Most men prefer a shaven or nice, closely trimmed vaginal region. Women nowadays, do keep themselves either nicely trimmed, shaven or waxed. You definitely can voice your preference to your lover. Though, do so in a nice, respectful manner. Do not belittle or bash! You don't want to make your partner self-conscious.

Again, flavored oils or gels can be used, if you are not use to performing oral sex. This is a way to get use to your lady's unique flavor. It's so crucial that these lubricants are safe for women's genital regions!!! You don't want her to obtain a bacterial infection from these, or from anything for that matter! Do your research or even ask a pharmacist or expert!

Many products in the market have high sugar or fructose levels which are NOT advised! Others may have petroleum-based oil content; again, stay away from these too! Most women are in the know about these, but if you do decide to purchase some on your own, please ask the store rep or better yet, ask an OB-GYN!

Another product that can be used is 100% pure grape seed, coconut, or olive oil. These are high in vitamin E, which is healthy for the skin and even vaginal linings. A little drop is all you need! HOWEVER, if you are using condoms you can NOT use these oils as they will break down latex condoms and latex sex toys. You need to use water-based or silicone-based lubricants with condoms. Now if you just want to get her off orally, by all means use these! They make terrific massage oils too.

It's a matter of choice and flavor preference in what you use. Providing oral pleasure to a woman, "typically" no lubricating product is necessary. However, regarding female lubrication, as women reach menopause, dryness is often an issue. Even with oral sex, a lubricant is advised to provide comfort. All ladies reading this, don't be afraid to teach your man about these aspects! It's your pleasure that we aim for!

Most men only concentrate on the clit during oral sex. Maybe men are taught this, as it's the most sensitive region on women's genitals. Sadly, many men dive right after it aggressively. Remember, men can be task and goal-directed creatures! During oral sex, men might not have a clue that other genital areas are sensitive and love being licked, sucked and perhaps nibbled too. Again, a woman's individual likes and desires must be taken into account.

Men are reading this and now looking confused while saying: *"Greg, what the hell are you talking about; there's only the clit and the vagina!"* 😊. Well gentleman, listen and learn, because you are so naive!

I'm going to first give you a little female anatomy lesson. There are more genital parts on a woman than just her clit and her vaginal opening. Have you heard of her labia majora and labia minor? These are the vaginal lips; and I would hope you've heard of these. They are sensitive as well and can be licked and lightly sucked on, providing great pleasure to most women. Do you ignore these and dive right for her clit? Stop! Kiss, lick and suck on her lips as a part of oral foreplay, thus keeping her anticipation building.

Now, as I said before, don't just dive in like you're a slobbering Saint Bernard! Women hate this and think you have no clue what you're doing! They're right!

Also, gentlemen, have you heard of the clitoral shaft, hood, or Mons Pubis? Yes, the clit is attached to the body by a tiny shaft that resembles a tiny penis. Many men have no clue this exists; well, many women don't either. Read and research these genital components. These can also be pleasured by lightly touching, caressing and licking. Let your lover's verbal commands and moans guide you to what pleases her, and also what kills her pleasure.

I am not going to cover every aspect associated with orally pleasing your lady in this book. That will be for a later addition. This is a simple guide for you to explore, and hopefully use to enhance your oral talents.

How many know that the very bottom of the vaginal lips, right above the butt hole is also sensitive and can be enjoyably licked? Additionally, the perineum can take a good licking as well. This is the region between the anus and vagina. Some old-schoolers refer to this as the *"taint"* in joking circles: *"Taint, the pussy; taint the ass; it's the little piece in the middle."*

During oral pleasing, the use of your fingers can either be a huge added turn on, or can totally annoy the hell out of your lady. Each woman is different, so ask and if she doesn't know, experiment! Some women love it as you are licking and sucking her clit, to have you finger her inner vagina. This is more of caressing the inner walls of her vagina: the sides and bottom, or floor region tends to provide an awesome feeling for her. Oh, and don't neglect the lips either.

Many men know about the infamous G-spot as well. This sponging tissue can be caressed with more finger pressure as you lick her clit and shaft. Practice and learn together what she enjoys, plus, what she hates. Pay attention to her body movements. Does she move into a certain touch, lick or sucking; or does she back away? Oh yes, even though I mentioned this a bit ago, she may love her butt hole licked or fingered too as part of the oral pleasing repertoire.

Building up pleasure through oral sex helps your lover embrace your touch, tongue and mouth! Your excitement in bringing her or him pleasure this way, totally adds to both of your sexual experiences and delights. Knowing what your lover enjoys, and paying attention to their body motions will pave the way to oral bliss. Each gender using verbal expressions is also highly recommended! 😉

Chapter 21: Sexual Awareness: A Snippet

Having a healthy sexual attitude often gets blocked by our insecurities and unhealthy beliefs, surrounding being a *"lady"* or *"gentleman."* I challenge you to work on your false beliefs. and begin feeling more open, and free sexually!

It's not just about the physical pleasures. Sexual awareness embraces the emotional and spiritual connection shared between two people who love one another. It's about learning to be vulnerable, to get rid of myths, and the *"bad girl or boy"* complexes.

Throw body image elements on top of this, and then you wind up having an unhealthy view on sexuality and sexual expressiveness. Maybe you are paranoid of being called a: a slut, whore, bad girl, dog, man-whore, hoe, skank, you name it. Allowing your sexuality to evolve to its fullest, doesn't mean you are any one of incorrect labels! It means you are more in tuned with your sexual mature self, plus have the confidence to express that sexuality to your partner! Ultimately, you know what you want sexually and you're not ashamed of that! Now that's fucking hot and freeing! As a human race, we need to rid the world of sex shaming against any gender, orientation, in any form, where mutually consenting adults are considered. Consent is the key word!

Do you ignore problems in the bedroom, as you do in your relationship? Well, typically if there are problems in one area, it affects the other. Though I didn't have to tell you this; did I? Even with it being 2020, people still have a difficult time talking about their sexual issues or challenges. I get it, it can be anxiety provoking, gut wrenching or embarrassing.

Typically, being sexually timid and insecure affects your relationship as a whole. It often is that proverbial elephant in the room. You are afraid to bring up that he doesn't bring you to climax. Perhaps he doesn't want to hurt your feelings by telling you that he's bored of you "just lying there." I do fully understand. It's not easy for most of us!

Has this been an issue for you? Again, I get it! These aren't easy areas to cover and often cause distance, hurt and angry feelings. Though, if you don't discuss these issues openly and calmly, they will come out in many unhealthy forms. I promise you that!

I want you to start being specific on exactly what you need emotionally to reduce these fears. Would it help if you received more positive affirmations, compliments, foreplay, or kind gestures? If you are waiting for these things to happen automatically in order to open up, chances are you'll be disappointed. When it comes to discussing sexual satisfaction and pleasure, people often wait before it's too late. Please be more proactive in expressing your wants and desires. It does get easier, I promise!

Because your lover wants to throw you up against the wall, rip your clothes off and fuck you, doesn't mean you're just a piece of meat. There could be great love and soulfulness involved as well. Being on the same page in how you feel sexually, is crucial! Because once in a while, you love it raw, doesn't mean love is left out of that act. Understanding this and what your sexuality is all about is crucial in promoting growth. It's a balance about how you feel about yourself, your partner, and your relationship sexually. Expectations about feelings, emotional, and the physical pleasure need to be expressed and clarified.

Many women feel like they're just a *"piece of meat"* sexually. Wait, some women love to feel this way! 😉 Those who don't; what are you doing about it? As you know, this ultimately kills your desire and sex drive all together. Are you communicating these feelings to your partner, or are you too shy or embarrassed? You deserve to be heard and understood!

First, does he have a clue what you mean by feeling like: *"just a piece of ass?"* He may not intend you to feel this way at all, and may just be attempting to showing his desire for you. It's your job to clue him in what you need, to feel loved and adored outside the bedroom as well! Of course, I don't let men of the hook here. Men need to start asking their partner if they are feeling loved or just like a piece of meat sexually. I'll keep doing my best to teach this. It's a crucial step!

Men must learn and understand what you need to feel important and valued; not just for your body! For many women to be sexually "free," there needs to be an emotional connection of love, appreciation and respect. These elements are needed to reduce the *piece of meat* feelings!

Descriptively tell him that you want him to hold or embrace you; hold your hand or caress you, and that it doesn't always have to lead to sex! Tell him you'd love it if he brings you flowers or writes a simple *"you're beautiful"* on a sticky note placed on the bathroom mirror. I'll do my best to teach men the physical and emotional connections needed to help women feeling desired and loved. Ladies, you need to help your partner become more attuned to your emotional needs as well. Don't hold back here!

Men, for the most part, need direction in getting clued in on the sensual aspects of sex. Again, the important element is to forget about what "other" women desire or want emotionally and physically! Be an individual and key in on what you want! Specifically touch on what he can do to make you feel loved and desired on all levels.

Men need to learn that all women are not the same, in their emotional desires surrounding sexual fulfillment! By him *"getting"* the sensual acts of emotional connection, you will start feeling like you're being emotionally seduced and connected once again. Do you remember those feelings of yester-year? The balance of emotional connection and being sexually desired need to be taught. Bringing up what "he" did years ago to make you feel fully connected can help as a guide.

Women, please pay attention here! For most men, sex is a way for us to feel desired, wanted, and loved. I personally get this from sex too! This means sex is an emotional experience for most men as well. Go figure, huh? LOL. I'm not lying ladies, nor exaggerating this aspect. I'm not here to blow smoke up anyone's ass. My passion is to help both genders get rid of the damn idiotic myths and sexual stereotypes we grew up with.

A huge part of this involves bridging the emotional and physical domains together, in what you both enjoy. It's not about what society or your parents told you about: *"you should only do this."* Focusing on the emotional experiences will create a deeper sexual awareness, thus creating more pleasurable sexual experiences on all levels. Overall, you will share a more passionate and loving relationship in general.

Chapter 22: Letting Your Freak Out

Have you been working on letting your freak out; or as one mature student suggested: eroticism? A part of this area was talked about in both the verbal expression and oral sex chapters. Though, I only hit lightly on the subject. Seducing one another definitely involves this aspect too, thus helps in allowing your sexual maturity to thrive! By *letting your freak out*, you are able to become more sexually open, uninhabited and confident. What do I mean by *"freak?"* Pay attention and I'll get to that shortly. 😉

What would it take to bring the freak out in you, and in your relationship? Now *"FREAK"* is subjective and can be anything from S&M *(Sadomasochistic)*, B&D *(Bondage / Dominatrix)*, to trying a new position or leaving the lights on. Letting your freak out doesn't have to be the extreme on the *"freakiness"* spectrum; well unless you'd like that! What would it take to bring the freak out in yourself and in your relationship?

Part of letting your eroticism evolve and being more open sexually, is the willingness to share your sexual fantasies. I am going to warn you! By letting all of your fantasies be known to your lover, there is a chance that you could be judged by your partner. I never want you to feel this way as you share your deepest sexual fantasies with your partner. HOWEVER, I'm being honest here. I wish there would no judgment and you could openly enjoy sharing your fantasies. You need to pick and choose which sexual fantasies you share, and which you keep to yourself. Hopefully you can feel safe in sharing them all! I will state this: as long as they don't involve hurting yourself or hurting others! It's about adult consent!

A lot of this has to do with your own confidence and having the attitude: *"Hey, these are my fantasies and there's nothing wrong with that!"* Sharing fantasies can be scary, though, is also a part of who you are as a sexual being.

It is important to note: Fantasies do NOT have to be acted out! No one should tell you they "should" be! This is a matter of comfort level within yourself and with your lover. Be careful too, that you know the consequences of acting out fantasies. Perhaps you desire a three-some or to engage in an orgy party. What could happen if these were acted out; feelings of betrayal, jealousy, or your lover getting emotionally connected to someone else. You need to think these through!

Another aspect could be legal repercussions. Say you have a sexual fantasy to get butt wild and have sex in the middle of the city park at noon. Well, you may get arrested. 😊. Sometimes just verbalizing your sexual fantasies is enough to tantalize you and your lover. You get to pick which fantasies you'd like to act out, and likewise for your lover.

You may have a fantasy of being tied up and tickled all over with a feather and want to try that. Engaging in an S&M sexual liaison may be a fantasy; however, that might be one you'd never want act upon. Or perhaps you might want to explore that? Simply fantasizing about it mentally, can be enough for you both. It's your choice, and that of your partner! Just have fun with it and explore these together. Boundaries and repercussions are important to discuss and reach agreements as a couple!

Chapter 23: Physical Pleasure

Embracing one's physical pleasure typically is what drives the sexual experience. I did cover some of the physical sexual pleasures in the sections on foreplay, and oral sex. These definitely can, and should be involved in the physical pleasures expressed through sex. Hell, most of us crave and love these, along with the "actual" penis-vaginal interplay. This part will not be extensive. It's only to highlight some key elements to explore, and hopefully enhances your sexual appetite and longings.

I get cracked up by mention of all the so-called "sexual positions" out in the world. There's the reverse cowgirl, wheelbarrow, flying-lindy. People brag about trying this Kama Sutra move or loving that Tantric one. Oh yes, this one too: *"We invented this or that position."* 😉 Yes, I'm laughing, not to belittle others, but out of enjoyment at the naivety that many have. Listen closely! Are you paying attention? There are only three main sexual positions! Four, if you include 69; and yes, I love that one too!

Now that I got your attention, and your mouths are flung open in disbelief, let's look at the three main sexual positions: 1) man on top (missionary), 2) woman on top, and 3) man-behind (doggie-style). Every other derived sexual position is a variance of these three, well minus 69. Do you understand? Let me give an example: throwing your lady up against the wall and fucking her is a standing version of missionary. *Reverse-cowgirl* is basically the same as woman on top, or doggie-style; mostly doggie-style (man is lying down versus "behind" her). The list of examples can go on and on.

I even touch on this subject while teaching college students in my Human Sexuality classes. I have them throw sexual positions at me trying to verify if my theory is justifiable. Well it's not "my" theory, as this has been widely known throughout the professional sexuality community.

I get the mystic and creativity in trying new positions and enjoy it myself. I just want to give you a run down on the facts. Each variant of the basic three may provide for extra physical stimulation, or allowing one person to take control of the pleasure, though remember the foundations. Certain angles of penetration can be more exhilarating to women; while others are to men. Most people already know this. The main aspect is exploring which is more pleasurable to you, and to your lover.

Physical pleasure can be a "quickie," or last for a while as you allow foreplay to be embraced, and your senses reach heightened proportions. Then as you feel you can't be pleased more, the "real" sex begins.

Try to see which positions bring the most pleasure! Can that hard cock hit a certain zone in the vagina that makes the woman moan in ecstasy?! Can it hit the deep spot, or brush her G-spot? Oh, my apologies; the deep spot is right before the cervical opening, and can be quite pleasure arousing for women. Often, this is touched during anal sex, or angling a little upwards during doggie style. Again, you do NOT want to hurt or damage your lover! Go slow when experimenting or trying anything new!

I often hear complaints about the lack of multitasking during sex. This often relates to a lack of touching and kissing. *"Greg, once I'm inside, she stops touching me;"* or *"He stops playing with my tits or kissing me when he's inside me."* Yes, these are actual client quotes! A huge part of the full physical pleasure experience is incorporating the foreplay acts into the main dish.

Do you touch, caress, kiss, even lick and suck your partner while “it’s” inside?” Does she like her neck bitten while your hard cock is throbbing inside? While you’re on top of him, does he want his nipples sucked or squeezed? What about her clit being caressed while you’re inside her? Damn, she can also touch her own clit! These gestures do typically increase one’s sexual satisfaction. Yes, some positions are tough to kiss during sex; I’m sure you get that…. 😉

You need to be responsible for your sexual satisfaction! Do not leave your lover guessing what you crave, or what you hate sexually. Don’t be afraid to verbally express in teaching your lover these elements. Though PLEASE, be caring in your approach and speak from your heart.

Here’s another subject that gets shunned or thought of as gross; anal or butt sex. While many frown upon the thought of anal sex, there are many who crave it, both men and women! Yes, there are a lot of women who enjoy anal sex. I mentioned about the deep spot. Anal sex can provide direct stimulation to this vaginal spot, bringing significant pleasure to women.

Some think of the anus as *"only an exit"* route, not an entrance. This is like any other sexual act, in that it's a matter of choice and preference. If you or your partner are curious and desire to try it, go SLOW! Very slow! I always advise beginning anal play with a finger, slowly around the outside perimeter, using a caressing and teasing motion. Again, go slow and also talk to your lover while inserting your finger a little bit. Make sure she, or he is comfortable. It's highly advised she expand her anus, as in defecating.

Only insert more of your finger based on her or his command! It's widely advised that you try a finger a few times so she can get use to the sensation and pressure. Only then, "should" you proceed using a penis, a sex toy, or butt plug. Many women need lubrication to help ease into anal sex. I definitely recommend it!

Anal sex can be quite pleasurable for many. In fact, there are many men who also enjoy having their anus fingered, played with, or "prostate milked." 😊. The anus and anal cavity have many nerve endings, thus can create significant pleasure. There's nothing wrong with liking this sexual activity. As always, you set your own limitations and boundaries. If it's not for you, so be it. That's perfectly fine!

Challenge your sexual beliefs, and where'd you learned them. Who decides if your sexual pleasure is "appropriate or "right?" You and your partner do! No one else. As long as it's consensual, not coercive, manipulative, or guilt tripped, it's fully up to you and your sexual delights!

Chapter 24: After Glow Connection

"Damn, that was hot, sensual, juicy, and totally body quivering! That's why I passed out after!" LOL. This section is going to touch on one element that tends to break not only the sexual connection, it dissolves the emotional closeness that sex provides. It's about the emotional disconnect that many feel after sex.

The *"After Glow Connection"* needs to be in place to keep the loving feelings flowing between you, your lover, and your relationship. Keeping this flow alive and going after the sexual act is over, helps you feel more loved and connected with your partner. Most complaints about this subject do come from the ladies. *"He won't kiss, touch or cuddle with me after sex!"* Don't get me wrong, there are women out there who don't embrace the after-glow experience. It tells your lover it's not just about *"getting off"* or *fucking*. It's about the emotional connection that highlights the physical pleasures just shared. Your lover won't feel like *"just a piece of ass,"* or it's just about the orgasm.

By staying connected after sex, you and your lover will feel more soulfully connected, cared for and cherished. So, after you both pee *(important to clean out the pipes and help decrease a possible bladder infection for her)*, caress and touch one another! Embracing and holding your lover are more than suggested.

Remember the section on verbal expression? This would also be a great time to implement verbal affirmations and compliments. Give compliments such as: *"that felt terrific, or you made my toes curl!"* More importantly, hit on the more emotional and loving gestures: *"I love how you love me!" "I'm so thrilled I married you!" "I love how you treat me, make me feel, appreciate or support me!"* You get the concept. Words, along with touching and embracing will help that after-glow keep burning; while bringing about a deeper connection that'll radiate outside the bedroom as well.

Chapter 25: Sexual Disappointment

Many people have heard about "Sexual Dysfunctions." I want to help break this injustice and follow the new school term: "Sexual Dissatisfaction" instead. Dysfunction is a cruel term attempts to determine a person having a severe deficiency as a person, or sexual being. This is sad and doesn't promote self-worth, self-love and destroys the full aspect of the person's sexuality.

For instance: A Man having "Erectile Dysfunction" can longer make love, or a Woman having "Pain Disorder or Dysfunction" is broken. Let's get rid of this unhealthy train of thought! Sexual Disappointment can come in all forms: pain, vaginismus, erectile, ejaculatory, and the list can continue.

It is crucial for any sexual challenge, be it pain, erectile, or low desire, that medical attention be sought. These situations could be the result of low testosterone, estrogen deficiencies, thyroid issues, blood pressure, medication causing symptoms. I want you to rule out any medical or biological potentials first.

Many people assume that a person enduring a disappointment can't perform sexually, give or receive pleasure. This is further from the truth! Can touch still feel good, kissing, oral sex? What about the benefits of emotional connection: does that go away if a penis isn't hard, or a vagina has involuntary spasms? Of course not..

I'm not naïve and do fully understand the emotional hurdles associated with sexual disappointment. One may not feel like a "Man," or a "Woman." I'm not saying this is easy! We can still make love by kissing, caressing, using our fingers, tongue and mouth. Even implementing sex toys into the mix.

We can stare into our lover's eyes as we perform oral sex, or use our fingers to gracefully deliver pleasure. The soulful connection can still be great. Implement the foreplay strategies and increase the verbal expressions of love, caring, and desire. Having challenges with out sex organs can be embarrassing, though we must remember our sex organs still include the skin, touch, words, and of course our minds.

There is even a Tantric aspect where a couple can make love via "soft-penetration." The man can guide his soft penis into his lover's vagina. Yes, this takes practice and certain angles make this more obtainable. Even with a soft cock, you both can feel a sense of closeness and some genital senses. This way, you both can also feel as close as possible physically and soulfully.

Often times, with sexual disappointment, one or both partners don't want to talk about the "issue." Talking openly can bring about an even deeper connection of safety and compassion. Be honest and sincere in how you both feel and offer suggestions as I noted in this chapter. Sex organs don't have to be the hard cock or wet vagina. Practice compassion and understanding, plus more importantly, the love you share for one another.

Sexual Endnote

The above sections on sexuality are to help enhance your sexual confidence, know-how, and pleasures. Again, I did not cover every single aspect, nor did I intend to. I did want to highlight some of what I consider crucial elements that I see with clients daily. I didn't touch on sexual challenges or issues, as those are too broad an area to cover in this book. It is wise, actually very much advised, to seek medical advisement should you experience any enduring pain, erectile problems or other issues associated with physical sexual discomfort. Make sure that you seek an OB/GYN, physician and/or a sexual therapist that is highly trained and experienced in sexual problems. Not all physicians, or even OB/GYNs are experienced in these domains!

By adding the above sexual dynamics into your relationship, I am hopeful these tools will reignite the sexual passions you both desire. You will feel more physically connected. More importantly, you will both feel emotionally cherished.

Part 4: Achieving Soulfulness

Chapter 26: Affair Prevention

Why would I write about affairs in the context of creating soulfulness? Because, sadly many couples, hell the majority of couples I have helped over the years have endured this devastating event. Affairs, both *minor* and *major* create so much hurt, anger, and destruction; yet at the same time can turn an emotionally and physically distant relationship into a passionate, loving and trusting togetherness. Sadly, this can never be guaranteed! Though, the odds can be positive.

I never, ever promote or condone affairs! So, please don't ever think affairs are remedies for reigniting your relationship! Work on your relationship or marriage before the wrath of an affair shatters it!

Affairs are often the aftermath of what marriages or relationships lack in one or more areas; predominantly the later. This is why I want to bring forth this topic as part of the soulful connection: because this is typically absent, misperceived, or not understood, and WHAM, an affair.

Have you been contemplating having an affair? Not getting your needs met with your current partner? Chances are you are feeling ignored, not desired, not listened to, taken for granted, not understood, or not important. Perhaps, a combination of these elements *(and it usually is)*. All these elements encompass the soulful connection.

Yes, I've talked about emotional connection, reigniting sexual passion, though creating a soulful connection is a separate entity that often gets missed, ignored, or never clarified. The soulfulness does encompass all of these elements, plus more. When this disappears, I believe relationships become despondent and begin to perish. Affairs are simply the escape mechanism often used by women and men to get out of a dead relationship, or put an end to suffocating.

Typically, both men and women who contemplate an affair, have longed for these cravings in their relationship for a long time. Most affairs occur because of these elements. (A crucial note however: not all affairs are results of these missing connections). There are some individuals out there who are chronic dogs or hoes, or are constantly seeking to boost their egos through sex. My heart goes out to you if you want to stay with these people.

It's my professional experience however, that 80% of affairs involve the missing emotional and physical connections. I won't speak for other helping professional with this percentage. It's only mine!

The main issue is why it happened? Many affairs happen for a reason, again I never condone or excuse this behavior! We need to look at the *"why,"* so it can be repaired; should both parties choose.

Many affairs occur because one (or both partners) has not felt important, desired, loved, appreciated or respected over time. In this situation, someone else starts paying attention, makes flattering comments, and let's be real, it feels good! A void becomes filled, thus leading ultimately, to indiscretions. These can be in the forms of an emotional, physical or a combination affair.

Just because I've stated *"many"* occur due to one of the above mentioned aspects, does not mean all do! Cheating and affairs have so much more depth to them than most people and other professionals realize.

As stated before, I never excuse or condone such behaviors! My work is to help couples regain the feelings and emotions they have desperately craved. Actually, many people desire those missing feelings from their current partner, and not from another, however……. Those having affairs just to build their egos or flaunt their prowess are a different animal.

In fact, I promote couples becoming stronger, deeper, and more intimately connected than they have ever experienced. Yes, it is very possible! I just wish couples would seek help for their challenges before an affair occurs. However, perhaps that's just my fantasy. I will keep promoting healthy love in reducing affairs none-the-less.

What to do after the devastation of an affair? Leave? Stay? It's very confusing as all the emotions swirl about: hurt, anger, sadness, killed trust, broken expectations, and low self-esteem. These emotions can actually affect both the betrayed and the betrayer alike. Here's a starting point I take with couples enduring such a heart-wrenching event.

There is no easy answer to rebuilding a relationship after an affair. Yes, there is and will be a ton of biased and judgmental answers to this question, unfortunately. I work with a ton of couples, and sadly, many have endured an affair. Shocking as well, is that just as many women are having affairs. In order to help couples repair, heal and rebuild, three questions need to be answered: *1) why it happened, 2) is there genuine remorse and guilt; 3) is there a re-commitment back to the marriage/relationship?*

The main issue is why it happened? In my professional experience, most (not all) affairs happen due to a craved element or elements missing in the relationship. Again, I NEVER condone or excuse this behavior! Though, we must look at this aspect as an avenue to start the healing process. Of course, that's if both parties so choose. I previously noted, that many affairs occur because one (or both partners) has not felt important, desired, loved, appreciated or respected over time. I know I keep repeating myself with the absent feelings. I'm doing that to drive home the importance of making one another feel these elements in your relationship. A void becomes filled by another person, thus leading ultimately to either emotional or physical indiscretions; often both.

Picking up on the affair topic: how many of you are able to take a look at yourself; really explore your actions, behaviors, or lack of action? This is separate, and definitely more growth promoting than blaming one other. It's taking responsibility for the state of the relationship leading to the affair. Again, because one of you was not feeling desired or loved, does not give them a right or free pass to cheat! This is to explore what broke down in the relationship, thus will help set the wheels in motion towards repair. Both must choose to heal from such a traumatic event, plus work their asses off at rebuilding trust, intimacy, desire, and passion. It is my hope that the relationship will be even stronger than ever thought possible. It does take work; a lot of work!

Learning to trust again is never easy. The betrayer needs to *"eat shit"* for a while. This time frame is very subjective for each couple and each individual. Themes like: *"It's been a month already, let it go"* won't cut it! The betrayer must still express remorse and empathy for the pain inflicted. If the betrayed partner asks to see your phone for texts message, email accounts, social media, etc., you openly show him or her! This is part of the shit you must eat at attempting to regain trust! The quicker you get this, and respond genuinely and openly, the easier it can be to heal and move forward.

One little caveat: the betrayed individual must also do their part to work towards giving the betrayer what was missing in the first place. This is never easy, especially when your heart has been ripped to shreds. The betrayed is rightfully so guarding their every essence from further pain.

It is crucial for me to be honest as well. The betrayer can to everything "perfect" to rebuild the trust, though, the betrayed may never be able to forgive and move forward. This is part of the battle and realizing that you want the relationship, and taking the risk to bust your ass in going after it. No regrets, or let's face it, further regrets if you were the one who betrayed.

I can do a complete book on affairs, alone. These are more or less bullet points, in helping you start repairing the aftermath of an affair. Most importantly, as with this soulfulness chapter, I'm trying like hell to help you prevent an affair in the first place.

Yes, there are those who are chronic cheaters, both men and women. It's your decision if you choose to remain in a relationship or marriage with these individuals. They cheat because of the thrill, to continually build their egos up, or what have you. There can be compulsive challenges as well. Though, sadly this term has been overused and exaggerated by the media and professionals alike. Be careful with this term!

An added note that's crucial to bring up: Those individuals or couples who practice open relationships, or who are in the "life-style" (swingers), or in a polyamorous situation are not cheaters! These are often consented to, and agreed upon within the couple relationship. Many people have misconceptions about these practices.

Affairs and cheating create devastation and shatters expectations and trust. With hard work, being genuinely remorseful and self-aware, these can be healed. Again, this chapter is not intended to be an all-inclusive tool to heal affairs, though to give you a few insights. I have also included a few tools at the back of the book, to help the healing process.

Chapter 27: What You Can Do?

Below, I'm going to attempt to write some important steps you can take in bringing about, and keeping a soulful connection. I broke these down into gender identifiers, though as most know, I don't buy into the hyped-up societal gender stereotyped roles.

Men: Pay attention to her, show her you still desire and crave her body and soul. If work or buddies take more precedence over her, she will: 1) find someone who will make her feel important, 2) will leave your ass, or 3) both. Stop taking her for granted! Express your appreciation and respect for her. Keep kissing her deeply and keep touching her sensually.

Don't stop telling her how much she is adored, loved, and that she is beautiful. Well, I don't mean every minute of the day, that would probably annoy the hell out of her, but you get the idea. 😊. Little gestures of appreciation as in notes, making her feel emotionally safe and secure go a long way. Take her out occasionally, just the two of you! Don't belittle or call her names (pet and bedroom names she loves are definitely okay! LOL)

Ladies: Don't take him for granted or make him feel like only a paycheck. Laugh and joke with him! Most men feel a deep emotional connection when being sexual with you; don't forget this!

If your man doesn't feel important and takes a back seat to your friends, the kids, or your family; he will distance himself. Guess what might follow; an affair as I mentioned in the previous chapter.

Do NOT stop showing desire for him! One of our biggest fears is that once we marry (or live with you), the sexual relations will dwindle and cease. This will make us feel not desired, not loved, being used, and tricked. Once we feel as such, we will pull away, leave, or find someone who gives us what we crave. I'm not saying a 24/7 thing at all, though, please pay attention.

Both: never stop talking; I mean deeply! Not just about the weather, work, or the kids. Talk about each other! Ask your partner if s/he feels loved and desired, plus accepted and appreciated. Make sure you make each other heard and respected! Stop being "too busy" for one another! If talking creates discomfort, then fight through that. By bringing that discomfort out in the open and saying *"it's not easy for me,"* will help actually decrease that fear.

These insights will help significantly reduce the possibility of an affair, the relationship becoming numb, thus ending! If problems are occurring in your relationship, I typically hit on 3 major issues. Most likely one, or more of these are neglected or missing:

1) feeling safe and secure emotionally
2) feeling connected and desired both physically & emotionally
3) feeling valued or important

Look at these areas first, in examining why there is a disconnect in your relationship. Remember, the above may not encompass physical or emotionally abusive relationships...although, how can you feel any one of the above 3 elements in that situation?

Self-responsibility! Are you taking responsibility for improving your relationship and sex life? Or, are you waiting for your partner to make the first move? So often partners wait for the other to reach out and take the risk first. They are afraid to rock to boat in fear of the relationship ending, or pissing each other off. Well, I pretty much guarantee that if the boat doesn't get rocked, you'll find out too late that the boat will sink!

Lovers become complacent, fearful of arguing and making things worse, thus, they stop talking. Please start talking deeply about your desires, hurts, fears and your genuine feelings; versus the surface bullshit stuff.

When the soulfulness ceases and we crave to feel connected, loved, and desired again, it may cause us to do stupid shit: like begin talking to someone on an intimate level. We typically don't even do this consciously! Someone pays us attention and makes us feel safe, then bam, the emotionally addictive feelings kick in. All along, we've wanted these very things from our spouses or partners, not from a stranger. The longings pull us towards soothing our pain. NOT a wise choice.....

What are you doing on a daily basis to show desire and love for your partner? Are you taking that risk, making effort, or are you just sitting back, relaxing and thinking it will just take care of itself? Additionally, what are you doing to improve yourself, make yourself more attractive, not only physically, but emotionally and intellectually? So many of us want our partner to grow or change, though we are unwilling to do so.

Chapter 28: Emotional Trust

Trust issues are a routine occurrence in my work with couples, not only sexually, but emotionally as well. I've talked on the topic numerous times regarding *"showing"* your love for one another; not just *"saying"* it. The first step is to get clued into what your partner needs to feel loved, and s/he requires. If you don't know, ask! It's important for both of you to be specific in your needs.

Words are often not enough, and can create contradictions. One's actions and behaviors may not match those words. When you say *"I love you,"* but your actions contradict those words, emotional trust begins to die. You need to be congruent with your words and actions to build, and maintain trust. You not only need to give your partner complements and verbal affirmations; you need to follow up with actions! Ways could be: *caressing, touching, kissing, love notes, and other little things that show they matter.* **Do these often and be genuine!**

So often, actions fall short from one, or both partners. I see the eye rolls, huffs, shoulder rolls when one partner says: "But I love you" to the other... The recipient rolls her eyes and shrugs her shoulders. Meaning, they don't believe those words and think they're bullshit. *"I hear you say it; but I don't feel it,"* are common rebuttals to the *"I love you"* verbalizations. "You say I love you, and that you are attracted to me, but you never touch me, want to have sex with me, and are usually a bitch to me." Tell me, how many of you have been in this situation before, or perhaps are currently there now?

Emotional trust comes by not only telling your partner you love him/her, you show them what they specifically need to feel it. This involves making your loved one feel important, valued, desired and crucial to you. Your lover needs to trust it when you tell him, *"You are important, loved, and desired."* It's NOT just hearing the words! Back it up with actions!

Each person is different in what they want, to feel and experience love. One partner may like to be shown with back rubs, or getting flowers. Others want the grass cut, or to watch the kids while she gets some free time. Learn what's important to him or her. Ask him or her; don't assume!

If you are being asked, tell them what you want, need and desire; and be specific! The more specific you can be, the easier it's for them to meet your needs.

Now, what if there's a constant reluctance to **"show"** the partner and excuses surmount....... *"no time, I'm tired, this happened, or that happened?"* My guess is that you'll be the one rolling your eyes when your partner says: *"I love you."* How long would it take before you stop requesting, or bringing this up to your partner's closed ears? How long would it take before you dismiss them and your relationship?

Trust can take a while to build yet, minutes or seconds to rip down! There are many other avenues to hit on related to trust and trust building. There's the level of trust during sex, where their partner "trusts" they won't choke too hard. Additionally, trust with doing what you say, being where you say, not gambling away the mortgage or rent payment, or to be there emotionally. The list can go on from there.

A very common trust issue erupts when one partner bashes the other, to friends or family. We all need to vent once in a while. Though, when you get into specific details and rip apart your loved one to others, trust dies. *"What did you say about me now"* tends to be a huge pattern that's created when this occurs. Be very careful in how you talk about your partner in the presence of others. Even if you are down-right pissed off, watch your words!

What can be done to rebuild the trust after it's broken? What's next after the proverbial, *"I'm sorry?"* Own your shit if you messed up! Reinforce your remorse and make sure you don't repeat the offense! Even if your lover doesn't receive your remorseful actions at that moment, don't get discouraged or frustrated. Be patient and keep being consistent! **Check in and ask your love what else can be done to earn back trust**.

I'm trying to provide these insights to prevent a breach in trust to begin with. Both must choose to heal from a trust injury. My passion is to help rebuild trust, create deeper levels of intimacy, desire, and passion. Not only rebuild these aspects, but make them deeper and more solid than ever thought possible. However, it does take both of you working towards one another.

Chapter 29: Questions of Care and Concern

A crucial element in making one another feel emotionally connected and understood is by asking questions. These questions are to implement concern, care and compassion. Let me be real, it's not easy to use these when we are getting screamed and yelled at. ☺ It takes practice.

Questions of concern are delivered to find out why your partner is pissed, hurt and simply what's going on with him or her. Most people may attack one another screaming: "You rotten SOB; I can't believe you did that!" Another could yell: "You pissed me off so much!" It's easy to fire back into the proverbial tit-for-tat battle ground, right? "Well, you pissed me off too!" I want this to stop!

When you start asking questions to gain knowledge and understanding, chances are your partner will feel understood. Thus, they are likely to stop yelling and speak from the hurt. An example: "What are you hurt about," or "Please tell me what I did to make you made." It makes it difficult for either of you to keep screaming at this point.

By asking with genuine concern, you are making your love feel important and cared about, versus a continued bashing match of who's right or wrong. Remember, the yelling and screaming may not be healthy, though underneath this, is the hurt or insecure feelings. Yes, I know it's not easy to ask out of concern when you partner is yelling at you. It happens, though by not firing back and genuinely caring about what your love is feeling, an emotional shift is created. A sense of "S/he understands."

Even if you don't understand what your partner is experiencing, you are tuning in to find out. Other examples of questions of concern can be: "I do care what you're feeling, please tell me what's going on." "I love you, and please tell me what you're going through, don't yell.

By asking questions of care, a sense of comfort is created and moves from the surface level anger, to the root of the hurt feelings. Both a huge plus! Many may be reading and saying, "Wait a minute Greg, you're saying it's okay that I get screamed at!?" LOL. No, no!!! I said it happens, not that it should be allowed.

Should the yelling and screaming continue, you have a right to say: "I said, I love you / care, though I can't listen if you continue attacking/screaming/berating me." "If that continues, I can't listen and will walk away." Then walk away if it doesn't stop. An added piece of advice would be to state: "I will love to hear what hurt you, so please come talk to me when you are able to stop yelling." Again, this continues to promote you care, plus also you don't allow yourself to be disrespected. I'm all about self-love and self-respect.

As with many of my helping tools and strategies, they seem "simple." I want things to be as simple as possible to make the biggest positive impact possible. I don't want to over-complicate things. Because they "seem" simple, doesn't mean they don't take practice. 😉

Chapter 30: "But We Have Kids!" / What's Your Relationship Teaching Your Kids?

Look deeply into your relationship. Is it the kind that you'd desire for your kids when they reach adulthood? I often ask this question to new clients. They look puzzled at first, then, expressions of shame and guilt run across their faces. As you might imagine, their answer to this question is a somber, "No."

I will preface their response and continue to challenge the couple by asking: *"Then what can we do to make it a relationship you'd be okay with for your kids?"* You see, kids tend to do as you show them. Monkey see, monkey do. Most of my clients and media followers are aware that I'm not politically correct; though attempt to build a bridge to happiness, love, health, devotion and passion for one another. Kids deserve too witness these aspects as well! Again, nothing is perfect.

Do you want your kids to be okay with constant yelling and screaming matches? What about frequent name calling, belittling and criticizing; or one of you being the bashing bag in these circumstances? Many couples endure these very aspects, yet don't realize the harm it places on their children. We get so caught up in our own pain, that we can't see beyond ourselves. I do understand this! Though, we must step outside of ourselves and explore how our relationship is affecting our children.

It's also a good thing for kids to see us making up after an argument. This instills we can disagree, make a mistake, and still love one another. It's a great gift to teach to children. However, as I noted above, what if these actions are constant and harsh? Then, it's not a healthy situation for anyone to be in.

Outside the arguing and name calling, a lack of affection, compassion and down-right coldness to one another is also unhealthy for your kids to exhibit. Perhaps there are no loving gestures shared, no verbal affirmations or appreciation shown. Your children will learn these attributes as *"normal."* I believe that's sad and cheats your kids out of what a relationship could, or even should be: passionate, close, affectionate, fun and loving. No, not perfect, but you get me.

Our fears may create a reason for us to remain in unhealthy situations; I understand. Fear of financial loss, not seeing your kids daily, loss of family and friends are all legitimate reasons. I've been there, and get you. However,

I'm still going to ask which is worse: your own personal fears; or the fear that your kids could end up having the same type of relationship you currently have?

Are you in a relationship where domestic violence embraces the household? Let me guess, you are teaching your kids to stick it out no matter what? A commitment is crucial after all! Yes, I'm being sarcastic here! Why not teach your kids that a commitment to themselves, and to love themselves is enough reason not to put up with such an unhealthy relationship?! That is something you can teach them!

The main premise of this section is to trigger positive growth and actions towards happy and loving relationships. What can you do to enhance the love, passion, and togetherness in your relationship right now!? Seek qualified help if possible. If it's beyond repair, what are you doing to get the hell out. Remember, your children are watching.

A side note here: preparation if needed if you do decide to get out of an abusive relationship. A place to go to, finances, the children's well-being all need to be taken into consideration.

Going back to my original question, with hopes the couple thinks at a deeper level: *"Would you want your kids to have the same type of relationship you have? Then what can we do to change it, or?"* I do promote that no couple should stay together for the sake of the kids. As you can tell, I believe unhealthy and toxic relationships damage kids' sense of what a healthy, loving, passionate relationship can and should be.

I'm not speaking perfection, but of working through problems. However, constant chaos is not healthy for any kids or for anyone. Nor, is your kids witnessing constant distance, silence, no touching, no embracing or no laughter. Again, I promote healthy, happy and passionate long-term relationships and marriages. This involves passionately attempting to rebuild that *total connection* for each couple. Unfortunately, that is not always possible.

I do promote a "no regrets" philosophy, where I'd like couples to try many aspects before calling it quits. There's no: "I wish I would've, could've, should've left. This is ever more prevalent when kids are involved. HOWEVER, when there is chronic violence and screaming matches, please take a break, separate, and get to a safe place away from these situations.

Chapter 31: Those Walls

I want to talk about walls that we've put up over our lifetimes. Those walls created from childhood traumas, abuse, being bullied, and having low self-worth. Then as we progress into our teenage years, our hearts get broken, we get crushed and embarrassed. Yet, we move onward. As the years pass, these walls start building taller, stronger and more entrenched. They become engrained into our personal essence.

As an adult, we are a little wiser *(so we think)* and open up again, then we get cheated on, ignored, left feeling alone, plus abandoned once again. We feel perhaps, not good enough, not attractive enough, tall enough, rich enough, you can add to this list...

Yet, deep down, we still long very much to be accepted, cherished, love and desired. We build all those walls strong and tall so we won't feel the pain again. Hell, it's probably causing the very thing we crave, to stay distant. It's that damn if we do, damn if we don't scenario. We want love, yet we don't want to get crushed again.

We stay guarded and protected, not allowing the one person who could be our dream to reach us. We keep them at arm's length. This also occurs in our relationships and marriages as well. A distance or chasm is created, and often we become fearful. Perhaps we lack the knowledge in repairing that crack. It could be all kind of reasons. Our fear sinks and empowers us to not trust, or open up again.

Being hurt and devastated, simply sucks! I fully understand that. Though, while you keep guarding against the getting crushed again, it stops us from very thing we crave. We safely repeat the mantra: "it'll never become possible, so why try." That loving and passionate bond you crave, keeps getting pushed away. Your fears of being hurt hold on tightly.

Let's face it; it's human nature to back away from the stove that burnt us. What people don't realize is that in working to protect ourselves, true love will never enter our hearts. Yes, it may be safe living this way, however you will go through life half-ass. I spoke on The Art of Relationships Show about this very element.

You can love fully and at the same time, be wise in loving and being true to yourself.

It’s these very walls that prevent us from reaching for the relationship we crave. That closeness we've longed for is held at bay as we numb out. *“It’s safe this way,”* right? Fears of getting crushed and devastated again, are held behind our wall of fear. It does take you to start risking again. You can be wiser and have greater knowledge and love better; plus, command the love you deserve. I want you to be strong, and open back up to your dreams of being loved and cherished.

Yes, it takes strength and confidence to be vulnerable and fully open to another. You can do it! It’s important to know that maintaining your strength, also means not allowing yourself to be toyed with. YOU can be fully open, yet YOU also command respect! Being vulnerable and confident at the same time is the key to the loving another and yourself. Trust your gut instincts, they are there for a reason. Do not ignore those red flags, or gut feelings, saying: “hey, something doesn’t jive here.”

Chapter 32: "Getting" One another

One of my crucial philosophies is trying to help couples "get" their partner. I get bewildered looks and blanks stares when I ask: *"Do you really get her?" "Do you really understand him?"* Smart ass comments typically follow: "*Yea Greg, I just give him sex and he's happy."* ☺ This may work, but isn't what I mean. LOL. *"Getting"* your partner includes understanding their moods, sadness, excitement, being tired or what have you. Not only noticing these elements, you need to be able to respond in ways that your lover emotionally needs.

For example: When your partner is angry, does he need to be left alone, or does he need a hug? What do you need if you're pissed off? Everyone is different in what they need, thus, perceptions are inaccurate. Such an example is: *"assuming"* what you need in a situation, must be what your partner needs. For example: when you're angry, you'd like an embrace and hear you're loved. Now, you automatically assume your lover needs the same thing.

In reality, you get angry when they reject what you "think" they, need (that hug and reassurance). Though, your partner gets further upset, and just wants space, and to be left alone.

Getting one another is not about what you would want in a given situation. It's what your lover does! Just because you need something, doesn't mean your lover wants the same thing. In times of anger, hurt or excitement, learn what your lover requires. Please start learning this!

Often, it's opposite of what you may need, maybe it's the same. Though, find out! Remember, this isn't about being right or wrong! It's about reaching your lover emotionally in struggling times. Your partner "should" be doing the same for your needs in a given situation.

Emotional support can be a tricky topic and one of subjectivity. It also goes very well with the above paragraphs. We all need support in our lives, especially when we our sick, exhausted, or have a friend that is dying from cancer. Do NOT *"assume"* your partner should handle difficult events like you would! Each one of us is different, and is a key part in "getting" your partner.

Some may want space and distance, while others desire closeness and affection. Learn your partner!

Misperceptions tend to permeate relationships: He gets bashed with *"Why are you being such a dick,"* as he's trying to joke around with his wife. *"Would you stop nagging me about taking care of the trash,"* as his wife constantly berates her husband as worthless. People may not be aware of what is going on inside of our partner. She isn't aware he is scared to death by a potential lay-off at work.

Nasty remarks happen, and are examples of misconceptions about what's really going on with our lover. These usually are avenues in feeling not heard, respected, or not feeling important. Defensiveness sets in, versus learning what may really being going on inside our loved one.

What if someone says: *"Greg, you're a dick!"* I want to learn why that person thinks I'm being a dick. If I end up verbally trash talking back *(I have before, I'm human. ☺)* it turns into an argument. It makes the situation worse and gets us nowhere. Getting in "tit-for-tats" is easy; not getting sucked into them is difficult.

This is where I want you to practice learning why your loved one thinks you're being a dick, bitch, lazy, anti-sexual, or you name it.

By wanting to learn, this will show your partner that you do love and care for her. Simply, your lover will feel that s/he matters to you. All of this content is a huge part of "getting" one another. Learn why, or what's causing a certain action or reaction. Try working on not getting defensive or reactive.

Being open and non-defensive is so important in learning what's truly going on. This involves paying attention to facial expressions and body languages. We get caught up in feeling disrespected and not listened to, that we may actually be at fault for not paying attention. I want individuals and couples alike, to stop the defensiveness and gain confidence. Start asking "what's going on," versus exploding back in a verbal tantrum. Remember, the chapter on Questions of Care and Concern?

Here's another example of a life event: A wife gets annoyed by her husband's bitter attitude towards her. He's short with her, rude at times and often ignores her. She responds to his attitude: *"You see why I don't want to have sex with you!"* He eagerly blurts back, *"like that would ever happen even if I was nice to you! You must be anti-sexual!"* Ouch! These verbal spears hit their mark and arguments typically ensue. This sadly, becomes the toxic pattern for many couples.

What's really going on here, and what would it take for this couple to *"get"* what's happening. You see, this wife's husband feels unloved, undesired and that she doesn't love him. Also, that he doesn't turned her on. All of his pent up hurt comes out in anger, disrespect, and you name it. Did the wife try to learn why he was treating her this way? Nope! She just was focused on her own feelings and emotions. He also may not have taken the time or insight to find out what his wife may be feeling or going through either. You need to start exploring what's below the surface, and not just what's expressed on the top level.

We can reverse this and look at the husband. Has he tried learning why his wife isn't as sexual with him as she used to be? Maybe she isn't feeling loved, important or perhaps, feels being taken for granted. You see, *"getting each"* other is about looking deep underneath what's presented. Don't just go by the surface shit! The key to getting each other is to learn what's going on at the root of the issues. Misperceptions are usually based on the surface level stuff (example: anger). By looking deeply at the inner most emotional levels of being loved, feeling important, being desired, and valued, we can avoid heated arguments. Learn to connect versus disconnecting further!

Regarding anger: most often a person exhibits anger and might yell, scream, get all red in the face, right? I talked about this in Questions of concern Chapter. Well, chances are anger is the secondary emotion to what's really going on such as: feeling disrespected, unloved, not desired, or not important.

By looking at the primary feelings, we are able to get at the "real" issue. Your partner will then feel understood and *"gotten."* This will catapult a reduction in further resentment and distance, which the typical tit-for-tat and bashing sessions create.

I believe that during these emotional events, our own insecurities come out. We start placing our own emotional needs ahead of our partners. That undying need to "fix things," or to make others "feel better" sets in and makes the situation worse. If we can't make things better, we tend to take this personal and get defensive.

Also, when our significant other is anger, we might want to run away or fight back. Feelings of insignificance, not being needed or wanted dart to the forefront. These feelings are about us, not our loved one's needs! By exploring our emotions and separating our insecurities from our lover's feelings, we will be better equipped to handle the anger and distance as they are presented.

Educate yourself in *"getting"* your lover. Does she need comfort or space after a bad day? Does he need to be brought a beer and allowed time to veg out after hearing his best friend is terminally ill? There are even times when our loved one doesn't know what she or he needs. This is perfectly fine. These are the times to not force *"fixes."* Be patient! A simple "I'm here if needed, or if I can help," can work miracles.

Chapter 33: Are Soul Mates Found?

I often get asked the question if soul mates are found, or, are they made. I want to cover this age-old belief, perhaps philosophy, throughout the world. Many people heard the stories of soul mates Romeo and Juliet, along with Anthony and Cleopatra. These so-called soul mates of love, or "twin flames" are what most of us long for. Well, minus the death part. 😊.

Remember back when you two first fell in love? You thought you had found your soulmate. As the years passed, you begin to doubt that your partner is actually your "soul mate." What happened?

Many people may answer this question, that soul mates are found. Then why is the divorce rate in the United States at 37-47%? Does this mean people settled and gave up on finding their soul mate? Perhaps, only married whoever was available? That's a sad thought!

I do believe that some soul mates are found, and I have been fortunate to actually witness a few. However, I believe that the majority of soul mates are made! Yes, most soul mates are made! My question is this: what have you been doing to make your partner your soul mate? Is your partner also doing the work to be your soul mate as well? Yes, initial chemistry, attraction and emotional connection needs to be present for a relationship to form. Arranged marriages being the exception to this.

It's my passion and goal to help you make one another, *"soul mates."* Okay, let me first say that nothing is perfect! 😊. Being able to looking at yourself and by applying the insights in this book, you can learn to become each other's soul mate. You will need to take responsibility for examining and working on your own flaws. Looking at these is a start, but you need to take ownership for your mistakes.

Most importantly, you need to be willing to work at reducing your disrespectful actions, and stop ignoring your lover's needs! It's ideal if your lover is able to do the same.

Soul mates work towards one another, not against each other. They create closeness not distance, while allowing and accepting that their lovers are individuals. Because you argue or disagree doesn't mean you're not destined to be soul mates! That's a relationship and life! A soul mate connection hangs tough through the challenges and is there for one another in mind, body and spirit. It's not the fairytale perfection that many people get caught up in. When reality sinks the fairytale dream, that's when people tend to argue, fight and begin pulling away. Stop this! Start reaching for one another in heart, mind, body and soul.

Remember to explore the underlying feelings of hurt, not feeling desired, important or valued. This will carry you a long way through the challenging times. It's one of the fundamental cornerstones in being your partner's soul mate.

Chapter 34: Is Your Heart In It?

For many who know, my logo is a specialized yin-yang symbol of a couple. It signifies the balancing hearts of love's true essence. I'm an Eastern philosophy buff, where dharma and karma intertwine into life balances of good and evil; pain and pleasure; ecstasy and crushed hearts.

As I wrote this book, I incorporated these philosophies, especially one is to put their heart fully into everything they do.

I believe that many in Western cultures bust their ass in their career and helping others, though do little work in their relationships or marriages. However, they expect great returns from their partner. Regarding love, we expect to give little of ourselves and expect to gain the great love and desire we think we deserve. It doesn't work this way!

Wake up people! If you think about it, we spend great energies and work protecting our hearts. This exhausted energy closes off the potential of the great love we truly desire. We get defensive, protective, and even attack at great lengths in order to prevent pain and heart ache. You don't even realize it, though you're *"working"* your asses off at guarding against heartbreak. In reality, if you actually placed effort focusing on loving, being open, and giving, you could have the love that endures. I spoke about these fears throughout this book.

As mentioned above, I'm a firm believer in placing our hearts fully into our work, our lives and especially into our love relationships. How can you fully give and be receptive of true love, if all of your work is centered on self-protecting, or centered on other life aspects?

How many of you have busted your ass going to college, working towards a job, or career you wanted? You might also work at helping your friends out in time of need, or at your favorite hobby. There are workaholics out there who are always chasing money, riches, or to have the biggest house. Think about this: does that big house actually make a home? No, it's the people inside.

It still amazes me that people are more willing to work their butts off in other life areas, though are lazy in their love lives. No wonder why so many people feel ignored, or not important to their significant others. Social media and cell phone apps pull us away from the person we love. We dedicate so much energy and time into these aspects, though ignore our love life. Why? Is it out of boredom, passivity or simple selfishness? I want you to start exploring your priorities and think about realigning them.

You need to be working at placing your heart in a different direction! Start staring more into your lover's eyes during and outside of sex. Kiss deeply more often, touch one another often, and actually listen to what your partner is saying. Start moving in the direction where you can be open and free to love, plus receive love in return. Work at receiving someone's heart and soul into yours.

Chapter 35: My Love Matters

A friend and associate of mine in the same office building made an awesome suggestion. Yes, this was a Sunday and I was actually at the office working on this book. LOL With all the chaos going in the USA during 2020, and the crucial importance of Black Lives Matter, "*Greg, why don't you promote "My spouse Matters?"* I loved this idea and wanted to start this great movement. I have forever promoted loving, passionate, and dynamic relationships though now, it has a solid name! 😊. But, wait a second……

Familiar feelings and thoughts came rushing in. These struck a nerve with me. Wait a minute! I work with a ton of couples who are not married. They may live together, be boyfriend and girlfriend not living together, or considered themselves partners, so perhaps *"spouse"* is too narrow and discriminatory.

"My Love Matters!"

I definitely wanted to expand the term *"spouse"* to include girlfriend, boyfriend, partner, lover, you name it! These all need to be included, hmmm, perhaps “My Love Matters” may be more fitting? Hmmm… Yes, better!

As people who follow me know, I'm all about relationships, building and enhancing our love lives! Having terrific, passionate, deep connected relationships is what I'm all about! Though, with numerous show episodes and blog posts covering the importance of showing the love you have for your partner, it still amazes me at how often people lack is this area.

So, come together with me and let's starts building this movement of *"My Love Matters!"*

I will start a series on this very topic with videos, Facebook and blog posts. It's kind of funny that I have always promoted these very things; like forever! LOL Now there's a title to it. Please help me promote this movement!

In Closing

I am hoping you're able to implement many of philosophies found in Love, Sex & Everything In Between: *The Relationship Guide* into your love relationship! By expanding your heart, soul and sexuality, you can start reigniting the passion into your relationship or marriage.

Be brave and remember, you are human and it's okay to screw up and not be perfect. Just own your goofs. Stop being afraid to open up your heart and love your partner. I mean really love him or her with each breath and gaze.

Re-read this book over, and use it as a fundamental tool in improving your own sense of self. Get rid of those stereotypes and taboos, that have been blocking you from what you've been craving your entire life!

Greg's Bio

Greg Dudzinski is a Licensed Professional Counselor (LPC) in private practice in Detroit, Michigan. His practice is called The Art of Relationships, PLLC. He specializes in relationship/marriage and sex counseling and is known as Love Guru Greg. Greg also has helped thousands of couples and individuals over 2 decades. He also has vast knowledge in helping clients through traumatic events, along with grief and loss situations. Greg is flattered and humbled to be helping others! He also hosts his own internet-based video show surrounding relationships and sexual topics: The Art of Relationships Show ©

You may contact him for speaking engagements, workshops as well as counseling services. Greg does in-person sessions, and also offers telephone and virtual sessions when appropriate. Greg can be reached at the following:

Website: TheArtofRelationships.org
Email: greg@theartofrelationships.org
Facebook: https://www.facebook.com/lovegurugreg
YouTube: LoveGuruGreg
TikTok: LoveGuruGreg
Instagram: LoveGuruGreg

Relationship Needs Assessment

Name:_______________

In order for our relationship to become more emotionally connected, I NEED these to be in place. (Be specific in your explanations! ☺)

1)

2)

3)

4)

5)

I need the following to be reduced or eliminated in order to feel more emotionally connected:

1)

2)

3)

4)

5)

What Can You Do Differently?

(Integrated with Dr. Ellyn Bader's Work)

Over the week, go home and answer the following five questions:

What type of relationship do you want to create? (Examples: "I want to create a loving intimate relationship, a relationship with more team work. I want a more affectionate, sexual passionate, empathic relationship, etc.")

How do you want to be as a partner? (Examples: How do I want to be: more affectionate, understanding, fun, humorous, Do I want to show my partner and family they are important to me, a better listener, that I don't always have to win or be in a competition with my partner)

What do you want to learn about yourself or the relationship? (Example: What do I do when I get hurt, or mad? How do I act (yell scream, or withdraw / shut down)? I really want my partner to know or realize, that at the root of my emotions, I am feeling: disrespected, unloved, undesired, etc.)

What do you want to stop doing? (Examples are blaming, name-calling, withdrawing, or avoiding conflict, anger outbursts, etc.)

What do you want to start doing instead? (Examples: "I want to stop blaming and criticizing. I want to start giving my partner more positive compliments or affirmations. I want to start saying what I appreciate and I want to start finding 'team' resolutions."

Limits to Conflict

In every couple's relationship, it is important to define the limits and boundaries of what is and what is not acceptable during a fight. Below, please define these limits for yourself in clear, specific terms. Also, define the limits you would like your partner to have. Be sure to cover such areas as physical behavior, voice tone, ending a fight and what you don't want said.

Name:________________________

*** Write what you both agree upon**

1) For us, it is acceptable to do the following during a fight:

____

____

____

____

2) For us, it is not acceptable to do the following:

____

____

____

(E. Bader – The Couples Institute)

:

Keeping the Love Alive

Kiss each time you greet one another when you are apart.

Cuddle every time you sit down together

Hug her/him every time s/he does something you enjoy.

If you haven't touched in an hour do so. Just a light touch can do wonders.

Rub one another's back

Offer a foot massage after work

Hit on, or flirt shamelessly with your person

Every time you feel that warm flush, tell her or him how much s/he turns you on.

Hold hands when you walk together, or sit next to one another.

Play footsie under the table when you are out.

Don't immediately cover up your body immediately after sex, or showering. Let your partner look and admire. 😊

^The above are only suggestions and you can come up with your own ideas to keep the fire ignited.

Relationship Dialogue

One thing I appreciate about our relationship?

One thing I dream about for our future?

One way I might get in the way of this dream?

What am I willing to do to create this dream?

One way I can ask you for help?

Sharing this vision with you, I feel?

One thing I appreciate about this dialogue:

(Tammy, Nelson)

Where on My Body	Stroking	Stroking	Rubbing	Patting	**Where on My Body**	Kissing	Licking	Sucking	Nibling
Head & Face					Head & Face				
Hair/Scalp					Hair/Scalp				
Cheeks					Cheeks				
Lips					Lips				
Ears					Ears				
Neck & Torso					Neck & Torso				
Neck					Neck				
Shoulders					Shoulders				
Stomach					Stomach				
Back					Back				
Buttocks					Buttocks				
Arms					Arms				
Elbows					Elbows				
Wrists					Wrists				
Palms					Palms				
Fingers					Fingers				
Legs					Legs				
Ankles					Ankles				
Feet					Feet				
Toes					Toes				
Full Body					Full Body				
Other					Other				

(Parts from Gina Ogden)

www.ingramcontent.com/pod-product-compliance
Lightning Source LLC
LaVergne TN
LVHW050642100826
845148LV00011B/1945

* 9 7 8 0 5 7 8 8 2 7 0 0 1 *